Mid

MADRID

THE NEW GUIDE
Michael's

MADRID

Managing Editor
Michael Shichor

Series Editor
Amir Shichor

INBAL TRAVEL INFORMATION LTD.

Inbal Travel Information Ltd.
P.O.Box 1870 Ramat Gan 52117
Israel

Intl. ISBN 965-288-113-9

Graphic design: Michel Opatowski
Cover design: Bill Stone
Photography: Yossi Shrem,
            Patronato Municipal de Turismo Madrid
Photo editor: Claudio Nutkiewicz
Editorial: Sharona Johan, Or Rinat, Lisa Stone
D.T.P.: Michael Michelson
Printed by Havatzelet Press Ltd.

**Sales in the UK
and Europe:**
Kuperard (London) Ltd.
9 Hampstead West
224 Iverson Road
London NW6 2HL

**Distribution in the UK
and Europe:**
Bailey Distribution Ltd.
Learoyd Road
New Romney
Kent TN28 8X

U.K. ISBN 1-85733-107-9

CONTENTS

INTRODUCTION

MADRID

TABLE OF MAPS

Preface

Madrid, Spain's capital, is a multifaceted and complex city, modern and dynamic. Visitors will be swept along by the enthusiasm and joie de vivre of the city, and will want to return again and again to stroll through the streets, admire the churches and palaces, and enjoy the atmosphere of its lively plazas.

Madrid is rich in history and culture. There are architectural gems, statues and paintings, world famous museums, quiet gardens, and interesting sites nearby for excursions out of the city. Its delicious cuisine, exciting night life and entertainment, both Spanish and international, will provide unlimited opportunities for your enjoyment.

In order to compile this Guide, our researchers spent months exploring the museums and historic sites, discovering exciting corners of the city, and investigating every neighborhood. They sampled the cuisine in a wide range of restaurants, and visited jazz clubs, bars and coffee-shops, in order to make recommendations.

We hope to introduce you to the many facets of this charming and dynamic city, and to put before you the opportunities which it offers. Our aim is to give you a deeper understanding of Madrid, to lead you to its best and most fascinating attractions, and to ensure that you derive maximum pleasure from your trip. We are sure that the effort invested in compiling this Guide will be justified by you enhanced enjoyment.

Michael Shichor

Using this Guide

In order to reap maximum benefit from the information concentrated in this Guide, we advise the traveler to carefully read the following advice. The facts contained in this book are meant to help the tourist find his or her way around, and to assure that he sees the most, with maximum savings of money and time.

The information contained in the Introduction should be read in its entirety as it will supply you with details, which will help in making the early decisions and arrangements for your trip. Reviewing the material thoroughly means that you will be more organized and set for your visit. Upon arrival, you will already feel familiar and comfortable with Madrid, more so than would otherwise have been the case.

The basic guideline in all "MICHAEL'S GUIDE" publications is to survey places in a primarily geographical sequence. The detailed introductory chapters discuss general topics and specific aspects of getting organized. The tour routes, laid out geographically, lead the visitor up and down the city's streets, providing a survey of the sights and calling attention to all those details which deepen one's familiarity with Madrid and make a visit there so much more enjoyable.

Following the tour routes, we have included a selection of "Excursions", which are all extremely interesting and worth a visit. Each of these excursions makes for a very pleasant trip out of Madrid.

A concise list of "Musts" follows, describing those sights without which a visit to Madrid is not complete.

The numerous maps which accompany the tour routes have been specially prepared, and show the visitor exactly how to reach the sights and attractions discussed in the tour routes. The maps will make your exploration of Madrid more efficient and pleasurable.

Madrid has a wide selection of regional cuisine, fine shopping and entertainment. Special chapters are devoted to "Making the Most of Your Stay" in the city. Here you will find a broad range of possibilities, which will help you enjoy your stay.

To further facilitate use of this Guide, we have included a detailed index at the back of the book, which lists all the major sights, and refers you to the place where each sight is discussed in greatest detail.

Because times change, and cities are dynamic, an important rule of thumb when traveling, especially to a vibrant city like Madrid, should be to consult local sources of information. Although we have made every effort to confirm that facts are up-to-date, changes do occur and travelers may find certain facts somewhat inaccurate when arriving at their destinations, and for this we apologize.

In order to be as up-to-date as possible we have included a short questionnaire at the end of the Guide, and will be most grateful to those who complete it and send it to us.

Have a pleasant and exciting trip – Bon Voyage!

PART ONE – A FIRST TASTE OF WHAT'S TO COME

Madrid, a City of Universal Appeal

Madrid, the capital of Spain, is a very special city. Unlike other cities, which developed through a natural process of events, Madrid was built expressly to serve as the capital of Spain, following the decision of King Philip II.

Madrid is almost like a mirage, an oasis in the wilderness of Castile. A first time visitor will form the impression that this sprawling capital seems to draw its vitality from the empty expanses around it.

Madrid is a dynamic and modern city, regenerating itself every day. Past glories are replaced by passing fashions, and even ancient vistas are liable to change.

Madrid is like a magnet for the people of Spain. They come from all the provinces to participate in the games of government and leisure. The inhabitants of Madrid are known as *Madrileños*, though few of them were born there. In 1853 Mesonero Romanos had cause to write: "Apart from the Queen, there is not one native of Madrid at the Royal Court – advocates from Galicia, Extremadura and Santander, physicians and merchants from Catalonia, poets from all over Spain..." The poet Antonio Machado wrote of Madrid at the turn of the century: "It is the whirlpool of Spain, the breakwater for 49 Spanish provinces..." The present King, Juan Carlos, was born in Rome, the Queen is Greek, the president is Andalusian and the mayor is from Syria... in short, to be a *Madrileño* means quite simply to reside in Madrid, no more, no less. Even the visitor can become a local, if he can adopt the right mood: a particular style of behavior which colors every one of

Plaza de España and the Gran Vía as seen from Torre de Madrid

Madrid's moments. Life in Madrid is a kaleidoscope of changing moments.

Spanish History

The Iberian peninsula, which includes Spain and Portugal, has been populated since pre-historic times. Caves containing paintings and tools bear witness to the existence of ancient civilizations. The first inhabitants of the peninsula were the Basques and the Iberians, and frequent waves of conquest and migration created Spain's complex cultural and ethnic fabric. The Phoenicians built the big Mediterranean ports, and the Carthaginians founded the settlements on the south coast. After a long and difficult war, Rome conquered the peninsula, thus paving the way for two hundred years of prosperity and development.

Large towns were built, roads were paved and rivers were bridged. For Rome, Spain was more than a colony – it comprised an important part of the empire, as is exemplified in emperors such as Trajan and Hadrian, as well as scholars such as Seneca and Martia – who were born here. Christianity reached Spain during Roman rule, brought in by Saint Pablo and Santiago, and by the time of the Visigoths conquest (466-484) it became the official religion of the country. With the end of the Roman era, Spain entered a lengthy period of turmoil and unrest. The Visigoth kings, whose capital was Toledo, were unable to control the peninsula.

In the year 711, various peoples and groups from North Africa, whose common denominator was their religion – Islam – began to invade the

Iberian Peninsula. Between 720-1002 the Muslims took control of most of the country. From the start of the invasion up to 1492, when Granada, the last Arab stronghold, fell, Spain endured a period of endless battles and struggles. In fact, these were not only battles between Muslims and Christians; in many cases, the two Christian kingdoms of Spain fought one another, with the Muslims allied to one side or the other. Despite the hardships, the arts, sciences and philosophy blossomed in the south, under Muslim rule. Muslim Andalusia was the home of the best of Islamic culture, a flourishing Jewish culture and the germinating Christian philosophy.

In 1469, Isabel of Castile married Ferdinand of Aragón, thereby uniting Spain. Under

FERNANDO EL CATOLICO

the rule of Ferdinand and Isabel, the "Catholic Sovereigns," the reclaiming of the peninsula (the Reconquista) was completed when Granada was conquered. Jews who refused to give up their religion were exiled, and Columbus reached America – all in 1492.

The old city walls of Toledo are a living testament of the rich history of Central Spain

The discovery of the "New World" across the ocean was followed by voyages of conquest which led, over the next few decades, to Spain gaining control of most of South America (with the notable exception of Portuguese Brazil), and all of Central America and Mexico. Spanish rule over Latin America lasted about 300 years, until the beginning of the 19th century, when most of the countries won their independence, one by one.

In 1504, after the death of Isabel, Ferdinand took over the rule of Castile. At that time, the country was at war with France. By conquering Navarre kingdom in the north-east of the peninsula (between France and Spain), Spain enlarged her territory. The kings of Navarre signed the Treaty of Valois with the French, and refused to allow Ferdinand's troops to cross their land. The Duke of Alba completed the conquest in 1515, and Navarre joined Spain under terms which are upheld to this day: autonomous public institutions, independent tax collection, etc.

The kingdom was expanding southwards, too. Melilla (in Africa) was conquered in 1487; Grand Canary in 1483; La Palma and Tenerife in 1445-1494; and Tripoli in 1483. At the time of Ferdinand's death in 1516, the kingdom included Castile, Aragón, Navarre, Catalonia, Valencia, Sicily, Sardinia, the Balearic Islands, Milan and Naples, most of North Africa, the Canary Islands and the colonies in South America.

Spain first became part of the Hapsburg empire (of Austria) during the rule of the Hapsburg ruler Charles V, Holy Roman Emperor (1519-58) who was also Carlos I, King of Spain (1516-56). He was the grandson of Emperor Maximilian I of Germany and son of Philip I and Joanna of Castile, and he inherited the Kingdom of Spain and its territories from his mother. The Hapsburg rulers did not succeed in winning over either the aristocracy or the people, especially after they attempted to introduce alien ideas and customs. Philip II, who succeeded Carlos I, directed his policies to one purpose: to place religious faith at the center of life. He waged wars to that end in Italy and Flanders, and it was

A monument to Philip II

The statue of Cervantes in Puerta del Sol

as a result of his defeats in those wars that the decline of his kingdom began. It was Philip II who established Madrid as the capital of Spain. Philip III inherited from his father the remnants of a proud kingdom, empty coffers and a backward industrial sector. He himself was weak-willed, and although he was the legitimate king, in practice the kingdom was ruled by the Duke of Lerma. Between 1601 and 1606, Philip transferred the court to Valladolid, then returned to Madrid. His son, Philip IV, a lover of the arts, patronized famous artists such as the painters Velázquez and Murillo, and the writers Lope de Vega, Calderón, Quevedo, Cervantes, Tirso de Molina and others. Like his father, he was not particularly well-equipped to deal with affairs of state, and he sought the aid of an adviser to manage political matters – the Duke of Olivares. His reign was characterized by sumptuous parties and celebrations, which were intended to hide the gradual decline. This situation continued during the reign of the last of the Hapsburg kings – Carlos II – who died at the age of 39.

The first Spanish king of the French Bourbon line, whose descendants sit on the Spanish throne to this day, was Philip V. During his reign (1700-1746), French influence was strong in the country. One of the reasons for this was that Louis XIV personally intervened to have Philip crowned. After the death of his first wife, Maria Louisa of Savoy, Philip married Isabella de Fransia, who was related to the Duke of Parma, and from then the predominant influence in Spain was Italian and not French. It was a time which saw the rise of England's strength as an empire, while the Spanish and French empires were declining.

Despite the deteriorating situation, cultural development was vigorous. The Royal Acade-

At the Palacio Real de Oriente

mies of Language, Medicine and History were built, as well as the Royal Carpet Manufacturers' factory, and the Madrid School of Surgery was established.

Philip V was succeeded by his son, Ferdinand VI, who married Barbara of Braganza. The central aim of his rule was to achieve peace and to this end he attempted to organize his country's foreign policy by making treaties with other nations. Historians agree that he was a well-loved king. His

A tapestry in the Oriental Palace

right-hand man was the Marquis de la Ensenada, who encouraged the development of agriculture and industry, and worked to restore the navy to its former glory. During the reign of Ferdinand VI, the Royal Academy of the Arts was completed.

Ferdinand VI was succeeded by Carlos III, his stepbrother, who was at the time King of Naples. Spanish society resented the fact that he brought new ideas from Italy and appointed non-Spanish ministers. His attempts to instil new customs and taboos, in an effort to change the way of life, (such as a ban on walking pigs through the streets, and various taboos regarding dress), aroused rebellion among the residents of Madrid. The uprising did not develop into a real revolution, but it did make Carlos III rescind his demands.

The rule of Carlos III was characterized by agricultural and industrial reform, and principally by wide-ranging cultural activity. Building was increased, especially in Madrid, in an attempt to modernize the city. Improvements were made in the sewerage systems and street lighting, and roads were constructed and improved. Carlos did not pursue his brother's peaceful policies in foreign affairs, and joined France in the Seven Year War.

Carlos IV succeeded the throne

Plaza del Dos de Mayo – the symbol of the conflict of 1808

in 1788. His court was made up of scholars and reformists. During his reign, Spanish society included individuals who were influenced by the French Revolution, and it was they who brought about the crisis in the regime. The immediate reaction of the monarchy to the French Revolution was to strengthen treaties with absolutist Europe, but in 1795, in Basel, a peace treaty was signed with France.

At the beginning of the 19th century, Spain was conquered by France and was involved in its own war of independence for six years (1808-1814). Napoleon held Carlos IV prisoner at Bayonne, and tried to kidnap his two young sons who had remained in Madrid. The attempt to abduct them forcibly from the city, on May 2, 1808, was the signal for the rebellion against the French, a rebellion which was quelled the next day with the execution of some of the rebels. Goya immortalized the killings in his famous painting, *The Third of May, 1808*. Despite its failure, this uprising symbolized the beginnings of the national struggle against the French.

On June 7, 1808 Napoleon's brother Joseph Bonaparte arrived in Madrid. He knew he did not have the support of the Spanish people, and reported accordingly to his brother. Napoleon, however, insisted on completing the conquest. Joseph Bonaparte was nicknamed in Madrid "King of the Plazas" for the many plazas and green spaces he added to the city.

At that time, 1810-1813, the Spanish parliament, the Cortes, convened at Cádiz, a city which had not been conquered by France, and legislated the "Consitution of 1812", a very

In the Iglesia de las Salesas Reales

progressive legislation which defended a free press and denigrated various feudal laws.

The war ended in 1814, and Ferdinand VII was restored to the throne after he was forced to renounce his throne and abdicate to Napoleon I (1808-14). During this period he was imprisoned and became a symbol of Spanish nationalism. He then introduced policies which displeased and disappointed the people, who had believed he would prove a liberal ruler. He abrogated the 1812 Constitution and arrested prominent liberals. The period of Ferdinand VII's rule is regarded as one of the most dismal in the history of Spain: universities and newspapers were closed, and some of the rules of the Inquisition were reinstated.

So after a prior period of relative freedom achieved through political process and internal pressures, absolutism had returned to Spain. In response to the request of the Verona agreement (Russia, Austria, France and Prussia), France dispatched her armies to the aid of the Spanish king in an attempt to squelch the discontent on behalf of his Spanish citizens.

The death of Ferdinand VII gave rise to civil discord between two new factions: the Carlists and the Isabellists – Carlists recognized Ferdinand's brother Don Carlos as the natural successor, as opposed to those who supported Isabel, his daughter. Isabel was still a child, and therefore her mother, Maria Christina, held the regency. In 1843 Isabel was crowned queen. In 1854, following an uprising, a revolutionary junta was set up,

which maintained a progressive government for two years. Then social problems began to emerge; the economy collapsed, factories were closed, and in September 1868 a revolution began. Isabel left Spain, and the Constitution of 1869 was instituted. Amadeo of Savoy tried unsuccessfully to rule for two years, and was finally forced to give up the throne.

In February 1873, the First Republic was proclaimed in the Congress and the Senate, but it lasted a mere two years. In 1875 Alfonso XII, Isabel's son, was crowned king. During his rule there was a period of stability, during which a new constitution was enacted in 1876. It lasted for over fifty years. Alfonso XIII was born in 1886 after his father's death. His mother was regent until he came of age, and then he ruled in his own right until 1936. He then left Spain upon the outbreak of the Civil War, not wishing to be the cause of bloodshed among his people.

Politically speaking, Alfonso XIII's reign was a tumultuous period. Between 1917-1923 there were some forty government crises, the economic situation was unstable and there was a drop in the standard of living, both rural and urban. The unrest which was felt in Catalonia and the Basque country (País Vasco) at the time is still evident today. The farmers of Andalusia demanded agrarian reform, and in September 1923, General Primo de Rivera seized power. Alfonso XIII supported Rivera's military dictatorship (1923-30). The subsequent dictatorship lasted for seven

Retiro Park – the monument commemorating Alfonso XII

years. Elections were held in April 1931 and the Left was victorious throughout Spain. The monarchy fell, and April 14, 1931 marked the beginnings of Republican rule.

This bloodless revolution led to the feeling that Spain had reached political maturity, and great changes were expected.

It was the Golden Age of discussion in the bars and in the streets. Hundreds of literary and political meetings were held regularly; Madrid talked, argued, shouted and created without pause for breath. This period gave rise to two generations of writers and poets, among them Valle Inclán, Pío Baroja, Galdós, Alberti, Lorca, Machado and Jimenez. At this time the bourgeoisie and

The massive façade of Palacio Real de Oriente

Bohemian elements flourished, one nourishing the other. Huge hunting and recreation areas in the center of the city, once the exclusive domain of the aristocracy, were now open to everyone.

Politically, however, the Republic was torn from all sides: by the *Falange* (the Spanish Fascist Movement, which was founded in 1933 and was close in ideology to Italian fascism), the higher echelons of the military, and the clergy on one side; by the anarchists and the communists on the other. In addition, there were the nationalistic Catalonian and Basque rebellions, which alternately flared up and died down.

In 1936 the struggle turned into tragedy with the outbreak of the Civil War. At first, the Nationalists, led by Francisco Franco, were weaker than the government; they had to enlist many men and bestow officer status to all the youngsters of the upper classes. With no industry, navy or equipment, their failure seemed inevitable, but they received aid and support from outside the country. The Republicans, on the other hand, had hordes of enthusiastic men at their disposal, as well as industry and a navy. Their superiority would have been promised – had they had enough time to organize the army, which was chronically undisciplined and riddled with anarchy.

In effect, Spain had various armies under various commands, and there was, of course, also external intervention: Mussolini's Italy provided planes, which enabled Franco to invade from the south (70,000 "volunteers" were paid by Franco and Mussolini); Nazi Germany sent communications technicians and planes for training in Spain in anticipation of the coming campaigns. The Republicans received limited Russian and International aid (from the International Brigades), but it amounted to no more than a few people and some crude, outdated equipment.

The cruel war in 1936 made Spain the focus of the hopes and disappointments of the whole world, and ended in 1939 with the Nationalists' victory. Franco, as leader of the nationalists, took power in 1939, and ruled Spain harshly. He controlled the country for almost forty years, from the time he was proclaimed by the anti-Republican rebels as head of the "national" state. His painful and slow fatal illness, which ended on November 20, 1975, marked the end of a period unlike any other among the nations.

Generalissimo Franco, as he was known throughout the world, was born into a poor family in El Ferrol, Galicia. He fought in the Moroccan war between 1912-1926. His military career, during which he was awarded almost all existing decorations, was brilliant. In 1926 he was Commander of the Legion, and in the same year, at the age of 33, he was promoted to Brigadier General.

While serving in Africa, he gained the reputation of being a tough and efficient officer and a good tactician, but no strategist. He strove to restore to the army the proud status of former wars. He was conservative, a devout Catholic and anti-communist. Liberalism, parliamentarism and free parties were for him synonymous with national division.

In 1928 Franco accepted command of the Military Academy in Saragossa, where he served until it was closed by the Republican government in 1931. Even though he lacked

the support of the Left and did not hide his identification with the previous regime, he filled central roles in the army: Commanding Officer in Morocco (1933-1934), Chief of Supreme Command (1935-1936), and General Commander in the Canary Islands (March-July 1936). One of his most important commands was the quelling of the Leftist uprising in Asturias in 1934. He carried out this task not out of a desire to defend democracy and the Republic, but rather to further his aim to involve the army in the suppression of the Left.

When the Civil War broke out, Franco did not rush to participate in the revolution against the Republic, despite his views. Following the victory of the "Popular Front" in the elections of February 1936, he decided, after some hesitation, on his plan of action: on July 18 he took upon himself the command of the rebel forces in North Africa. The revolution led to a brutal and protracted civil war, in which some 500,000 died, hundreds of thousands became refugees, and the country was brought to ruin. The "nationals," as the

rebels called themselves, emerged victorious.

Franco's ambition was to establish a regime which had in it no place for political parties and trade unions. He wanted a kingdom, not in the liberal-parliamentary style but a traditional Catholic kingdom. He united the forces that had supported him during the war to form the "National Movement" (Catholics, Falanges and Carlists, supporters of the Don Carlos royal line), and in effect founded a regime of one political party and one leader. Thus Francoism was born.

Franco's forty years of rule can be divided into three periods: the totalitarian (1939-1945), during which 300,000 were incarcerated in prisons; the National-Catholic (1945-1956); and the technocratic (until 1975), which was also a period of development. Franco himself defined his rule as "the authoritative rule of national unity".

In forty years, Francoism turned Spain from a poor agricultural state into a modern urban and industrial society – but the price which the Spanish people paid for these changes was high.

Despite the criticism leveled at Spain by Western nations because of her identification with fascist regimes and with the Nazis, the Cold War between the superpowers rescued her from the international isolation she had suffered since 1945. In 1953, Spain gained the support of the U.S.A. in exchange for military favors such as the building of American bases on Spanish soil.

Economic progress began only in the sixties, when the regime introduced a small measure of economic liberalism – an ideology which did not fit very well with the aims of the "National Movement". It was then that the opposition began to appear, the very opposition which led to the slow collapse of Francoism. This collapse was accompanied by the deaths of thousands of Spaniards, who paid with their lives in bitter fighting against Franco's supporters, who tried to prove that they were as strong as they had ever been.

In 1969 Franco appointed Prince Juan Carlos as his successor, despite the objections of the prince's father. In 1975, following Franco's death, King Juan Carlos ascended the throne and legitimized all political parties. In 1977 free general elections were held. Democracy had become a fact.

King Juan Carlos undoubtedly stands as a central figure in the process that Spain has undergone in recent decades. He has stood firm against the attempts to subvert democracy, and his importance lies in his being king of all Spaniards, which in a country that has suffered

internal strife throughout the ages, is a fact of enormous significance. The problem of the various ethnic groups in Spain has not yet been solved, although it has been blunted somewhat by the establishment of autonomous entities (Navarre, Galicia, Catalonia, and the Basque country). The best formula for maintaining relationships between an autonomy and central government has not yet been found, yet today more than ever before, there is a feeling that Spain is on the right road despite all the problems. In January 1986 Spain joined the European Community, and her voice is increasingly heard among the peoples of the world. There are many who see a model and an ideal in the change which is taking place in

Spain, in the transition from tyranny to democracy and freedom, a transition which has since been called "the Spanish miracle".

Madrid – Historical Background

Madrid became Spain's seat of power during the time of the Muslim rule, when the Ameer Mohammed I (852-882) built the Almudena fortress on a hill near a stream. On the ruins of this fortress the Alcázar castle was built for the Christian kings, and when this burnt down the present palace was built in 1737. The Arabic name for the place was Maherit, and etymologists think that the name is a combination of the word *Mahra* – a well or spring, and the plural word-ending "it". The location was chosen both for the hill, a good defense spot in the area, and for the abundant water.

In 1083, King Alfonso VI decided to return Toledo to the Christian fold. On his way there, he conquered Maherit, thus terminating the Muslim rule which had given the town its name and its fortress. At that time, Madrid was an agricultural village surrounded by fertile fields and forests where bears roamed free (which explain the city's emblem). Madrid of yore is symbolized by San Isidro, the city's patron saint. Isidro was the servant of a wealthy farmer, who dedicated most of his energies to worship and prayer.

Philip II's decision of 1561 to set up his court in Madrid was a total surprise. His father, the Emperor Carlos V of Germany, (also known as Carlos I of Spain), was one of Philip's principal detractors. He wrote to his son from the retreat where he spent his final years: "If you desire to expand your kingdom, move the court to Lisbon; if you wish your kingdom to remain as it is, stay at Voliadolid. But if your desire is to destroy it – take your court to Madrid". Nevertheless, Philip designated Madrid the capital, and as the town came alive, he left for El Escorial, the monastery-palace he had begun building for himself in 1563.

We can assume that Philip's decision was based on Madrid's central location and the fact that the town was not involved in the rivalry between the bigger Spanish cities, but it is possible that Philip also had in mind reasons of personal convenience, such as its proximity to the planned El Escorial, or the fact that

Madrid was surrounded by huge expanses of forest promising ample hunting.

And so, in 1561, the hub of the kingdom moved to this little village. The move had a negative influence on the area: entire forests were cut down to provide timber to build palaces and houses for the new population, which suddenly grew at an enormous rate; the sun's rays dried up the newly exposed ground; fertile fields became arid and barren. The town grew in an unplanned, chaotic and thoughtless way, until the king tried, somewhat late in the day, to put things right and improve the town's appearance. Madrid owes to this initiative the Segovia bridge, built to bestow a grand entrance to the town. The lack of proportion between the spectacular bridge and the stream meandering beneath it led the playwright Lope de Vega to say: "Madrid should either buy a river or sell a bridge". The Plaza Mayor, Madrid's central square, was also begun about this time. This work was completed by Philip's successor.

The period of the Hapsburg dynasty of Austria, which ruled Spain from 1516 to 1701, is considered to be a time of prosperity. The arts flourished – especially theater, which was very popular with the town's inhabitants.

In the *Corrales* – very modest courtyards – the great plays of Lope de Vega, Tirso de Molina and Calderon were first performed. The simplest people went openly to the theater, while the nobles wore cloaks and masks, as such entertainment was not considered suitable for the artistocracy.

This same period brought tremendous development: the number of inhabitants, which

In Plaza Mayor, Madrid's main square

The Retiro

Alcalá Gate, the Prado Museum and the Botanical Gardens were built. Even before this, the wealthy citizens of the town had cultivated elegant tastes and added to their homes magnificent and ornate façades in the style called "Castilian Baroque".

The 19th century was ushered in by the thunder of the cannons of the French forces positioned in Madrid. On May 2 1808, the citizens of Madrid rebelled against the invasion of Napoleon's army. The mass uprising failed, and the emperor's brother Joseph Bonaparte ruled the town despite the open hatred shown

had been 20,000 in 1556, reached 100,000 by 1665. City walls were built and torn down four times to accommodate the town's unbridled growth; a few public buildings and many monasteries were built; vitality and tumult became order of the day.

A bloody war of succession led to the coronation of King Philip V, first of the Bourbon line (to which the present King, Juan Carlos, belongs). During this war, Madrid sided with the Bourbons, and when the new king arrived in 1701, he was enthusiastically received. King Carlos III (1759-1788), known as the "Mayor King" dedicated much of his time to improving the town and its life style. Madrid experienced vast growth – wide avenues were paved, the

towards him. Joseph Bonaparte was also enchanted by the town, and contributed much – especially the building of plazas. In 1813 he was obliged to flee, but managed to take with him many treasures and works of art.

In 1814 Ferdinand VII returned to Madrid, and the Toledo Gate was built in his honor. The constant growth of the city was again a problem. There were 280,000 residents by the middle of the 19th century. A new expansion plan was approved, and new avenues were paved. There was a strong French influence on the style of the day, and many buildings were built with verandas ornamented with iron trellis-work – a style very characteristic of the city.

Madrid entered a new era at the beginning of the 20th century. In 1919 the city Metro was opened – one of the first in the world, and the Gran Vía was laid and paved. It is still the main thoroughfare and heart of the city.

During the Civil War, Madrid, seat of the republican government, was a stronghold for the regime's forces against the nationalists. The city was mercilessly shelled by Franco's forces.

Franco's regime raised more than one monument in a style popularly known as "fascist architecture". The most prominent of these is a collection standing in Plaza Moncloa: *Ejército del Aire* (Air Force Command), the Plus Ultra memorial, dedicated to some of the war's victims, and Franco's Victory Gate. It is well known that the planning of this monument was supervised by Albert Speer, Hitler's architect.

By the 1960s, about two million people lived in Madrid, and many new middle class neighborhoods were built. Circling the city were neighborhoods occupied mostly by Andalusian immigrants seeking

In the Real Armería

employment. These places have become centers of makeshift huts and illegal building. In order to solve the problem of public transport to and from the city, first class roads and underground parking lots were built.

Today, Madrid has a population of about four million and is the undisputed center of activity and of modern Spanish renaissance.

Geography

Madrid is both the political and the geographical center of Spain. It has the highest altitude of all capitals in Europe (2,000ft above sea level), situated in the region called the Castilian Plain. There are no precipitous mountains nor huge rivers; streams and wadis outline the city's general lines.

Madrid is situated half way between the River Tajo and the Guadarrama range. It spreads to the foothills with sandy and alluvium soil on one side and irrigated land on the other, the former yielding wine, the latter wheat and olives. The hilly areas are covered with pasture land and woods, and near the Jarama and Henares rivers, vegetable gardens abound. The abundant underground water in the area formed clay, which is a good building material, and wood and granite found on the mountain side are also a rich source of building materials. All these factors together created the best possible conditions for the building of a city. When Madrid became the capital, its rapid development almost ruined the region's ecology, but the problem was solved by a network of approach roads constructed in order to bring from afar the things missing in the city and its environs.

At first, Madrid expanded between two steep valleys, one which is today in the area of Segovia street, the other further north, at San Vicente Hill. The Guadarrama range is the city's northern border (maximum height 8.000 ft.); in the southeast it is the Jarama river, into which Madrid's river, the Manzanares, runs. The character of the city is divided into two: the part facing the mountains, and the part overlooking the valley. The former, the more northern of the two, is wealthy and elegant; the latter is the "worker's town", more modest and industrial. In recent years, the slopes of the hills have become vacation spots; the inhabitants drive out of town by the thousands for the weekend, and many have

second homes there. There are also several ski resorts.

Climate

Madrid lies far inland, and is cut off by mountains from moderating maritime influences, so there are big changes in temperature between the seasons. In December and January the average temperature is minus 5°C, and between June and September it is over 20°C, and can reach 40°C. Average annual rainfall is not very high – only 430 mm. Rain falls mostly in spring and autumn, but there are also occasional summer rainstorms, which pass quickly. These are basically convectional rainstorms, but precipitation is also increased as moist winds rise up the mountain slopes.

Population

Madrid has grown quite rapidly during the 20th century. Its 576,000 inhabitants in 1900 increased to 1.1 million by 1940 (and this was after the Civil War which claimed it's victims). Today some 5 million people live in the entire autonomous community of Madrid, 13% of the Spanish population. Renewed planning of economic resources, public services, building etc. became necessary in view of the expanding population.

Between 1948-1954, new dis-

tricts, previously classed as villages, were added to Madrid. Most of them sprang up alongside the main roads leading to the city. In the few short years, the districts of Aravaca, Hortaleza, Fuencarral and Chamartin were added in

the north; Canillas and Canillejas in the east; El Pardo and Villavaro in the west, and Carabanchel Alto and Carabanchel Bajo in the south.

Spain's serious economic problems were particularly felt in the rural areas, and caused many crises. These led to a process of internal migration from the poor districts to the more developed and dynamic locations where employment could be found. From 1950 until today, approximately one and a half million people have come to Madrid, mainly from Andalusia, Galicia, Extramadura, Castile and Asturias. Apart from Madrid, places such as Valencia, Catalonia and the Basque Country also absorbed large numbers of migrants. In addition, about a million people left Spain for other European countries, finding work mostly in the services. This vast migratory movement brought Madrid's population to over three million by 1970. Madrid attracted people for many reasons. It is the second largest industrial center in Spain, and the management levels of the private sector are concentrated here. About a third of Spain's large companies are located here, and in the seventies the most prestigious office blocks were built in the Paseo del Castallana, Orense, and Colón districts. At the same time, new housing developments were built expressly for middle and upper class newcomers; luxury developments were built in the northern sector of the city, and in fact, only the city center remained unchanged. Builders and contractors provided work for thousands.

In the seventies there was also an influx of immigrants and refugees from other countries to Spain, and to Madrid in particular, who were attracted by the new democratic spirit of Spain. Most were motivated mainly by economic factors but a considerable percentage came because of political upheavals in their own countries. Principal among these are Filipinos and South Americans. There is also a large group from Africa (mainly from Guinea) and smaller groups from Arab countries, especially Morocco and Iran. Exact numbers are difficult to determine, as many of them are living in Madrid illegally. Gypsies are another large group, almost all of whom live in appalling conditions on the outskirts of the city, and make their living from peddling,

trading scrap and begging. Unemployment in Madrid is high, especially among young people and newcomers, and crime has increased accordingly over the past few years. The changes in population and life style in the city have also brought polarization among the city's residents. Madrid has quickly become a real metropolis, with all the advantages and disadvantages involved: economic prosperity, a wide range of creative possibilities, entertainment and development, on the one hand, and increased demand for consumer goods, rising crime, loneliness, and the breakdown of traditional frameworks on the other hand. Nevertheless, there are still some village-like areas which perpetuate the old way of life: the rural migrants tend to hold regular meetings, and there are many associations which record and preserve the characteristic customs and traditions of each district. On the numerous festivals and holidays that the Spanish enjoy, many people go back to their villages.

One of the most serious problems facing Madrid is that of the younger generation. In addition to unemployment, a new phenomenon is growing – the breaking of traditional frameworks. Spain is essentially Catholic, but the Church's influence upon young people has waned drastically. In Franco's time, youngsters could either seek refuge under

the Church's wing, or be active against the regime. Two things happened when Franco died: firstly, there was a decline in the importance of the religion, and secondly there was a decline of values attributed to political activity. These two processes caused – and are still causing – indifference among the younger generation to their personal and collective futures. A grave expression of this situation is the rate of addiction to hard drugs, which has reached alarming proportions in Madrid. Tremendous efforts are being made by the authorities to combat the drug problem, for example, the opening of youth centers all over the city, which offer a wide variety of activities.

Another growing sector is the 35-45 age group, educated outside Spain. It is this sector which is presently running the country both economically and politically. They have a particular life style, setting the tone in Madrid. They live outside the city, take pride in their appearance, and dress in expensive casual clothes. They eat and drink only in moderation, even though good food and drink are traditionally considered one of the main pleasures of life in Spain.

These are the inhabitants of Madrid – a multitude of nationalities with different ways of life, with contradictions in every sphere.

Government

The King is the head of state and commander-in-chief of the armed forces. On the surface, it would seem that his authority is extremely wide, but in fact it is strictly limited by laws which govern the shape of the democratic regime. The Spanish government is the King's government, but the people elect it. The King's signature may validate the laws, but the authority to discuss legislation belongs only to the *cortes* (parliament) and the government.

Every four years general elections are held for the congress and the senate – the two houses of the *cortes*. In the senate, every constituency is represented by its four elected officials (about four representatives per province). The sessions in both houses take place from September to December and from February to June. When the elections are over, and after consulting with all the parties, the King proposes a new president to the congress. The Congress debates the suggestion for two months and then votes.

In addition to the central institutions, Spain has regional institutions, whose role is to regulate the autonomous regime based on the constitution. It is well known that Spain is made up of several nationalities, peoples and cultures. For forty years Francoism had suppressed every attempt at self-determination, under the slogan "for the sake of the unity of the Spanish people". All these bans were lifted when Franco died, and

The Spanish Congress

forbidden languages were heard anew on the streets, on the radio, and on television. Public institutions renewed their activities.

Each autonomical entity has an independent government and parliament, entitled to suitable sums of money from the national treasury. Among other things, the autonomous government attends to public building, housing, road building, the building of ports and airports, commerce, education, agriculture, water, fishing, culture and language, tourism, health, social work and local police.The Spanish police force is a very complex entity indeed, and it is easy for the outsider to become confused. Not only are there several police forces each with its own uniform, but their authority and areas of activity differ from one another. There are the national police (in brown), the city police (in blue), the civil guard (with black hats called *tricornio*), and several other autonomous police forces – each dressed in traditional regional garb.

Alongside the government institutions there is a Public Defender (*Defensor del Pueblo*), to whom citizens may turn if they feel their rights have been abused. This office is usually headed by a public figure acceptable to all the parties, a fact which lends him a dignified image and assures his objectivity.

Spain has a Constitutional Court which enjoys full autonomy, standing above even the Supreme Court. It is elected by the congress and consists of twelve judges. Every three years, one third of the judges are changed, meaning that each judge can serve a maximum of nine years.

Political parties (as well as others) can apply to the Constitutional Court in cases where they feel that the parliament has enacted laws which contradict the spirit of the constitution. There have been times when the Constitutional Court has considered central and controversial subjects such as the Abortion Law, the Education Law and others.

The Cultural Scene

Recently, there have been many changes in Spanish

society. Franco's death and the decline of his regime have opened the cultural, economic and social possibilities of the western world before Spain.

For many years, Spanish artists wanting to be involved in the cinema or theater were obliged to go to France or England. The end of censorship has brought new life to these spheres, and cultural life is enjoying a renaissance. Neighborhood parties and local clubs are no longer the only option for the younger generation; the rebirth of cinema, theater and art has opened new doors.

Spanish citizens need only I.D. in order to enjoy free entry to museums, and many families combine their Sunday outing with a visit to a museum where, in addition to the permanent exhibitions, there is a wide range of alternating exhibitions centering on contemporary foreign artists. One can also see traveling exhibitions from the world's most important museums, including, in recent years, exhibitions displaying Spanish art in all its forms. Not only government offices are active in this project, but also public institutions and the banks.

One expression of the importance attached to the arts is the wide use made of the works of the artists in advertisements for government offices, municipalities etc. No self-respecting municipality is without its annual art award or graphic design competition for its town festival.

It is said that the Spanish are particularly romantic. If a people's romanticism can be

Cine Doré – cinema is one of the favorite pastimes in Madrid

36

In the Museo del Prado

measured by the number of its poets, then the Spanish are indeed romantic: every year thousands of books of poetry are published, financed by the poets themselves, by public funds, or by various awards. The situation is somewhat different with prose writing. The newspaper kiosks are flooded with cheap editions, and most of the world's literature is translated into Spanish.

While Spanish literature has not succeeded in regaining its former glory, there is a new generation of writers in evidence. The children of the Civil War are having to compete with the foremost writers of the century – Lorca, Unamuno, Pio Baroja, Alberti and others. Some of them have returned to Spain after long periods of exile, during which they fought for many years to have their books published.

Today's literature reflects the changes which have come about in Spanish society. One now finds new confrontations with more personal and intimate issues, and characters totally without hope. The "black novel" in Spain not only has a wide readership, but has also brought to the fore some very good writers. A considerable number of writers have found the press to be a good medium to express their opinions, and thus have given rise to a new form of journalistic writing.

Because of the paucity of important modern playwrights, theaters mostly present the plays of classical writers. However, new centers are coming into being, which try

to stage the works of young writers who are influenced by the new trends in world theater. One of the areas traditionally deeply attached to the theater is Catalonia, where the most important of the companies can be found. There are

The Gran Vía

several festivals during the year the most significant of which is the Madrid festival, usually held in March. These offer good opportunities for companies from all over the world. The town festivals are an excellent opportunity for amateur dramatic societies, which appear in the plazas and at other outdoor sites as well.

These festivals are also the framework for the rock, hard rock and punk music concerts, whose popularity has risen among Spanish youth as it has worldwide. Hundreds of groups have been formed lately, largely influenced by the English, Americans and Germans. There is a big difference in the music popular with the people of the housing developments and the suburbs

and that enjoyed by those of the wealthier sector.

The "older" generation prefers a different kind of musical entertainment. The over-30's can be found at the jazz festivals (Madrid and Bilbao are the best), or in the pubs where small jazz combos, both foreign and local, appear. This same audience comes to hear the singers who had already gained fame in the 70s, such as Serrat, Aute, Sabina, Ana Belen and Victor Manuel. These singers usually write their own words or take them from the best of Spanish poetry.

In the field of classical music, Madrid is still far behind the other great cities of Europe. It has no opera house worthy of the name, and it is very difficult to get tickets for the concerts of the national orchestra or visiting orchestras from abroad, which are held in the Royal Theater (Teatro Real). Modern music is also sorely lacking. One of the most popular types of concert is the light music played by the municipal orchestra every Sunday during the spring and summer in the Retiro Gardens.

Every year Madrid holds opera and ballet festivals in the Zarzuela Theater, but these spheres are not particularly highly developed.

The Zarzuela is an original Spanish genre which combines

the spoken word with music and dance, largely influenced by the Viennese operetta. Many of the works in this genre have been inspired by Madrid's history: *La Verbena de la Paloma* (The Festival of the Dove), *La Gran Vía* and others. Few new works are written in this genre today, and, in fact, the Zarzuela belongs to Spain's nostalgic and impressive past.

Cinema, however, is a highly popular form of entertainment. Madrid has over a hundred cinemas, and the more modern ones are housed in the comfortable and magnificent buildings. The worldwide rivalry between the cinema and television and video is familiar here too, but the Spanish enjoy an evening out. Spanish films are of excellent quality, as the prize winning films shown at international festivals bear witness. Until recently, all foreign films were dubbed into Spanish, but these days efforts are being made to change that system, and there are now some cinemas which show films in their original language, with subtitles.

Architecture – Periods and Styles

Spanish architecture carries traces of the different peoples which dominated the country.

Some constructions have been demolished and rebuilt in a different style throughout the course of the years. Others have been modified according to the style of the different periods.

Spain has one of the most famous prehistorical paintings in the Altamira Cave. A copy of the painting can be found in Madrid. Traces of inhabitants of the paleolithic epoch can be found in other parts of the country like Galicia and near Grenada.

From the Roman epoch there remains several aqueducts; among them the one of Segovie which crosses a whole neighborhood and dominates the city from a height of 100 feet. Traces of the Visigoths can only be seen in the region of Toledo. The buildings are made of freestone embellished with overstepped arches.

With the Moorish Conquest came the building of mosques and the predominance of Spanish Moslem style in architecture.

The horseshoe shaped arches of the Córdoba Great Mosque are typical. People worked at

Segovia Bridge, the impressive entrance to Spain's capital city

the building of this edifice throughout two centuries (785-987).

In the Asturias which didn't go through Moorish invasions, a style called pre-Roman appeared from the 8th century until the 11th century: simple and massive churches like the Ancient Royal Palace of Oviedo, which later became Santa Maria de Maranco Church. The 11th century gave birth to the Mozarabe phenomenon.

Mozarabe people were christians living under moslem domination. From this period many churches situated in the Provinces of Leon and Castille can be seen. At the same period the Mudéjar style appears. Mudéjars were moslems taken in the Christian Conquest. Their art is characterised by the brick construction embellished with glazed clay mosaics.

Among the edifices built during that period: the Alcázar of Seville, the Alhambra of Grenada and the Synagogues of Toledo (later transformed into churches.) Those two architectural tendencies remained dominant until the 15th century.

Roman art also developed during the 11th century, in the north of Spain at first, then in all the peninsula.

Vast churches and citadels with big arcades and vaulted ceilings were built. Those churches can be seen mainly in the region of Leon and Compostelle.

Gothic style appears in the 13th century. Born in France, this art remained dominant until the 16th century. At the beginning it was not accepted easily in Spain. It is characterised by broken arches, high bays and buttresses. It can be appreciated to its full when the light shines through the stained glass windows of Leon Cathedral.

Gothic style developed into Isabelin style which is characterised by numerous details showing military deeds, historical and religious events.

The plateresque style dominates the 16th century – the ornamental work which looks like that of the goldsmith's trade is typical of this style. Less care is taken for the structure of the building than for the ornamentation of its decorative columns of wrought iron.

Juan de Herrera is the most outstanding character of Spanish Architecture in this century. (He is the architect of the Escorial of Segovia Bridge in Madrid.) He influenced the emergence of the Italian Low Renaissance.

At the beginning of the 17th century, encouraged by the monarchy, baroque style made its appearance in Spanish architecture. The monarchy tended to centralize its power and, in order to express its authority, it used its artists. Thus, enormous palaces, theaters and other edifices were erected. baroque style can be divided into two periods: the first one from the beginning of the 17th century is the most restrained; the second one, from the middle of the century, expresses joy and victory. baroque architecture

Moorish influences in a Jewish synagogue at Toledo

Cibeles Square and the Communications Palace

was fashionable until the 18th century and, as years went by, ornaments become more and more abundant and elaborate. Edifices built by Ribera – like Madrid Town Museum – are an example of this period.

Ornamentation in architecture became so rich that it made the line of the building itself. Enormous exotic rooms were built and gardens with uncon-ventional perspectives were fitted out. Other artistic forms like tapestry, porcelain and embroidery also flourished. Superb examples of those can be seen at the Eastern Royal Palace (Palacio Real de Oriente).

Rococo, a style which originated in France in the 18th century, didn't last long in Spain. With the discovery of

Pompei and Herculanum, a new style took over: neo-classicism. Mythological images – Greek and Roman pop out from everywhere: fountains, statues and paintings. Architecture became more restrained, classical foundations and well balanced dimensions became fashionable. Villanueva's buildings (Charles III's architect), are good examples of this style and can be seen at the Observatory and at the Prado.

The National Library built at the beginning of the 19th century is a good example. Romanticism bloomed in Madrid and took on new shapes. Everything is "neo" in architecture: neo-baroque, neo-Mudéjar, neo-Gothic and others. Architects of this time drew their inspiration in folklore, to create balustrades and verandas embellished for the houses they dreamt of and built. In contrast, the monumental style was being born, principally represented by the Communication Palace (Palacio de Communicaciones).

By the end of this century, a new concept emerged: art nouveau. Gaudí is its best representative, especially in Barcelona. A good example is Rongovia Palacio in Madrid where essential characteristics of the modern stream are identifiable: curved lines; abundant use of glass and ceramics and smooth shapes.

Damage caused by the Civil War and cultural isolation didn't help to create favorable conditions in architecture for the 20th century. The principal aim was the relocation of the "homeless" Modern constructions worth noticing are the Palace of Congress with its façade of Miró, the enormous commercial centre – Madrid II; the Vaguada with its avant-garde architecture and the Mercado Puerta of Toledo which is next to the Flea Market.

Painting and Sculpture

Painting began to flourish in Madrid in the 17th century

which is considered as the Golden Age of Spanish painting. The greatest painter of this time is undoubtedly Diego de Velázquez (1599-1660) whose paintings of the countryside and portraits are considered unsurpassed. He skillfully portrayed the realism and atmosphere of his time. Italian influence is cardinal and Italian artists played a role in the configuration of the "Madrid of that time".

Velázquez, painter of Philip IV's court, was twice sent to

At the Prado Museum, where classical beauty catches one's eye

Italy, and brought back beside the knowledge he acquired, a beautiful collection of paintings which decorate the Royal Palace to this day.

By the second half of the 17th century a new "school" developed marked by the Flemish influence of Rubens and Van Dyck with a tendency to precision and details whose Spanish representative is Juan de la Corte. Sculpture also reached new heights at that time.

Sculptors were specially attached to religious subjects – their wooden-images are very typical of Spain. The two representatives of this artistic genre are Pedro de Mena and Luisa Roldan.

In the 18th century, Flemish influence was eclipsed by the French influence, this due to the change of Monarchy. Rococo style became popular among Spaniards who added their own stamp to it. This style suited the lovers of fantasy, and the charming and superficial temperament of the aristocrats of that time. Furniture; ceramics; decoration and elegance in great detail were all characteristic of this style. In painting, romantic scenes with frivolous ladies of the Court in pastel shades were very popular.

If Rococo was only an ephemary style, its elegance and charm gave birth to a genius: Francis Goya (1746-1828). Goya's first paintings were taken as models for tapestry. They were full of joy and light. Goya doesn't belong to any school. His complex personality expressed itself in a number of his pieces, transcending all limits. He painted religious subjects, portraits of the king Charles IV and of the royal family (where we can distinguish a hint of criticism), a series of paintings and engravings depicting the disasters of war, showing the popular uprising of Madrid's inhabitants against the French, and the executions which followed, the black paintings that he performed during his old age, the expressionism (well ahead of its time) and the sensual, marvelous *Maja Desnuda* exhibited at the Prado.

During his life, Goya depicted his time and the people of his time with a creative strength unequalled until Picasso. At the beginning of the 20th century, many groups from the intellectual bourgeoisie introduced in Spain the avant-gardist schools of literature and plastic arts which had taken hold in other European Countries.

Impressionist painters appeared in Spain: Zuloaga, Sorolla – as well as modern painters like Pablo Picasso (1881-1973). He used all sorts of materials for his multiform work (oil, painting, collages, ceramics, etc.) which is divided into a number of periods: blue and pink periods (1901-1905), cubism (1906-1907), neo-classicism (1920), surrealism (1925-1936), and expressionism (1937).

Expressionism and surrealism flourished with Miró (1893-1985) and with the Marquis of Pubol, better known under the name of Dali (1904-1989). Salvador Dali, the last giant of surrealism, painted his first painting in 1910 and finished his last pieces in 1983. He has created the method of "Critical-paranoia".

The lovely rich interior of the Los Jerónimos Church

However, because of political and social insecurity raging at the time, avant-gardist painters left Spain for Paris. During the Second Republic cultural life had a brief resurgence but it ended with the Civil War. The Museum of Contemporary Spanish Art exhibits the development of Painting from the beginning of the 20th century until today.

Tradition, Festivals and Customs

Even if, at first glance, the *Madrileños* seem to have nothing in common with one another, they share an attachment to the many historical places in the city, which are their common background.

The most startling meeting of the old and the new is at the Rastro – a huge market held every Sunday. The crowds are enormous, like a human sea. Among the many stalls you can find almost anything – furniture, valuable antiques, leather and iron harnesses in the best punk tradition, bullfighter's clothes, second-hand clothing, works of art from Peru and Ghana, *galabiyas* from Morocco, new and old work tools, dogs, cages, and much more. The market spreads through a maze of alleyways, at the center of which stands a statue of the hero of the Cuban War, Eloy Gonzalo, holding a jerrycan of gas (with which he set ablaze an enemy stronghold) and looking down serenely on the goings-on around him. If you don't like crowds, we recommend that you come before 11am. The antique shops and some of the second-hand shops are also open during the week.

Madrid's most important festival is that of St. Isidro, patron saint of the city. It falls on the second half of the

month of May, when the city turns into a bustling fairground of theater, music, dance, bull-fights and street shows of all kinds. It is the official begin-ning of spring; the city offers a huge variety of events and you can enjoy yourself until the small hours of the morning in the plazas, parks and streets.

Every district in Madrid has its own saint, and throughout the year each district celebrates its local saint's day, which means that there is no time of year when there are no festivals. St. Antonio de la Florida Day is the main festival, celebrated on 13 June. From all over the city, young men – and some who are not so young – come to the church to look for a suitable bride. The evenings, of course, are, in the best Spanish tradi-tion, devoted to dancing, eating and drinking.

August 15 is the day of *La Virgen de la Paloma* (The Virgin of the Dove). This festival is deeply rooted in the folklore tradition, signs of which are still clearly visible. One of these is the *chotis* – a mischievous dance whose rhythm recalls the tango, although it is less dramatic. It is danced in typical Madrid dress: the lady wraps herself in an enormous embroidered shawl called a *mantón*, and wears a red carnation in her hair and a white kerchief on her head; the man wears a close fitting black and white checked jacket, a white scarf around his neck, and a beret

pulled down over his forehead. Music boxes play, and the huge bowls of "lemonade" are prepared, but the contents are not nearly as innocuous as the name.

On November 15 there is another festival – that of *La Virgen de la Almudena*, the other patron Saint of Madrid.

The end of winter is celebrated with the Carnival. During Franco's regime the Carnival was forbidden, but since his death, after 40 years of restraint, it is celebrated with great elation and verve. Apart from the costumes and the parties common to Carnivals the world over, Madrid has some special ceremonies of its own, such as the "Burial of the Sardines" towards the end of the festivities. The origin of this custom is apparently an event which happened in the dim and distant past: a catch of sardines once went bad due to a sudden heat wave, and the citizens of the town reacted in the light-hearted way so characteristic of them, and buried the sardines with great pomp and ceremony, while quaffing great quantities of wine, as the occasion demanded. Today the ceremony consists of a procession which accompanies the coffin, the marchers being giants and clowns in macabre costumes whose dominant colors are black and purple. There is also a symbolic battle between Señora "Cuaresma", who symbolizes the 40 days' abstention from meat which separate the Carnival and Easter, and Señor "Carnal", symbolizing carnal desire. To the dissatisfaction of all present, the Señora wins and the Señor is tried and executed. And thus end the festivities.

Semana Santa (Holy Week), which is Easter week, is celebrated with a religious procession. Spain is strongly Catholic, and this festival shows clearly the strength and depth of religious feeling in the country.

In the summer and fall, the municipality organizes music, dance and drama festivals, with local participants and world renowned artists.

Finally, at Christmas and New Year, the whole city is lit by colored lights. On the last night of the year all the inhabitants congregate at the Puerta del Sol (Sun Gate) opposite the big clock in the tower, and every person eats twelve grapes – one for each chime: Champagne flows, congratulations are bestowed, as well as kisses for everyone within reach.

Olé! – The Bullfight

Even confirmed animal lovers probably arrive in Madrid with an embarrassing and secret desire to see, at least once in their lives, the *corrida*, the

Bullfighting is Spain's most famous fiesta

bullfight. Many tourists come to Spain dreaming of the exotic and colorful battle between the *matador* and the black bull, the red cape, and the red flower given by the black-eyed Carmen. In fact, although the bullfight is a national fiesta – it is a highly controversial issue among the Spanish. Many of them would like to ban bull-fighting but many others are addicted to it, considering it an art form. It combines great beauty and not a little cruelty, and it's worthwhile knowing that and being prepared for it in advance. *Tauromaquia* – the art of bullfighting – is by no means easy to master. It has its own special language, which describes every movement that takes place in the arena. Many writers and painters have been inspired by the spectacle. Hemingway and Picasso both loved the Fiesta, and it is a major theme in many of their works. The bullfight is a long established custom, its story rooted in the dawn of history, but its present form took shape about 200 years ago.

The *corrida* progresses through several stages. The first stage is the dressing of the *torero*, the bullfighter. This is an important ceremony which takes places in front of a small and select audience in the *torero's* dressing-room. His costume is called "the garment of lights", and it is indeed colorful and sparkling. It is exemely close-fitting, empha-sizing the fighter's body. He wears a black hat, and has a braid down his back, which he is supposed to cut off on the day he retires from the arena.

Next is the prayer ceremony. Before entering the arena, the *torero* prays to his saints. The ceremony is full of religious and even magic symbolism. There are many superstitions attached to the *corrida*. It is well known, for instance, that

if someone puts a hat on the fighter's bed while he is dressing, it's a very bad sign indeed. After the prayers, the bullfighter goes out to the arena, the Plaza de Toros, holding his cape, which is in itself a work of art in embroidered silk.

The biggest bullfighting plaza in Madrid is the Plaza Monumental de las Ventas. This is an impressive building in the neo-mudéjar style, which seats 23,000. The Plaza also contains a bullfighting museum, Museo Taurino, which one can visit before the fight.

Once all the spectators are seated, silence falls. The president takes out a white kerchief, the trumpets sound, the drums roll. All the participants in the celebration enter the arena, some of them on horseback. To the music of the *paso doble*, they circle the arena bowing their heads to the president, their hands on their hearts. They then exit the arena to change their ceremonial capes for "battle capes".

One of the youngsters receives, from the president, the key to the enclosure where the bull is waiting. He opens the door – then runs away as fast as he can. Fanfares and drumrolls mark the entry of the bull. Several youngsters, usually apprentices, attract the bull's attention giving the *matador* (the *torero* who will perform the "duet" with the bull) time to look him over. As he changes his cape, the entry of the *picadores* (lance-bearers) on their horses is announced with another fanfare. They stick their lances into the bull's back, to get him angry. Now the matador also thrusts some lances – called *banderillas* – into the bull, taking more risks than his helpers.

The battle between the matador and the bull is based on the tension created by the movements of the man and his cape, and the element of danger. The audience estimates the matador's proximity to the bull and the sharpness of his movements. Every successful contact is applauded with an enthusiastic "Olé!" When the fighter feels that the right amount of time has passed, he looks for a specific spot on the bull's back and plunges in his sword.

If more than ten minutes have gone by since the beginning of the *corrida* and the bullfighter has not yet killed the bull, the president notifies him by waving the kerchief. If he has fought well and bravely, his prize is one of the bull's ears, or even two ears and the tail. A bull that bests the bullfighter is put out to pasture and lives a long life – but this rarely happens.

We have already mentioned that popular opinion is not unanimous regarding bullfighting. Throughout history, there have been people who have opposed it because of the cruelty to a helpless animal. Many articles have been written – and are still being written – on the issue. Needless to say, the bullfighter is also exposed to very serious danger.

Bullfights are held from 28th February until mid-October. The Plaza Monumental de las Ventas is at 237 Calle Alcalá. The metro stop is Ventas, and tickets are available at the Plaza on the day of the *corrida*, and from agents at 3 Calle Victoria (Metro: Sol).

PART TWO – SETTING OUT

When to Come; National Holidays

The first question one asks is, of course, when is the best time to come. The answer, however, is not clear-cut. If you ask 20 different *Madrileños*, you will get as many different answers. Some will tell you that summer is the only time to visit, because then the city is almost empty except for a few Scandinavian golden blondes. It's very hot, however,

Violet blooms at the Jardín Botánico

in summer, and many places are closed, especially in August. A popular new summer fashion has developed in Madrid – a city vacation. In the evenings, the cafés are crowded, and there is a summer festival with theater, dance and movies in the open.

Others will warn you never to come in summer and say that winter is undoubtedly the best time to visit. It's true that

Madrid in winter is full of life. Just 60 km away there are beautiful ski resorts, and in the evenings the places of entertainment are lively and the traffic never ceases. The cold does get to your bones, but indoors it is well heated. There are also the winter festivals, and from December 20 to January 6, the city is alive with colored lights and universal merrymaking.

Spring is also a good time to visit – the weather is pleasant, and the city has many festivities with accompanying events, but don't forget your umbrella. Autumn is breathtaking in its beauty. Shades of red, orange and yellow are everywhere, the weather is superb, and the city seems to come to life again after the summer vacation. Needless to say, fall has its festival too. In short, each season has its own particular magic.

In addition to Sunday the following holidays are observed in Madrid:

January 1 – Año Nuevo (New Year)

January 6 – Día de los Reyes Magos (according to Christian tradition, the day on which the Magi saw the infant Jesus)

March 19 – San José (holiday of St. Joseph)

April – Semana Santa (the Holy Week)

May 1 – Día del Trabajo (Labour day)

May 2 – Liberación de Madrid de los Franceses (the day Madrid was liberated from the French)

May 15 – San Isidro (holiday of the Saint)

June 18 – Corpus Christi

August 15 – Asunción de la Virgen (Day of Ascension of the Virgin)

October 12 – Fiesta Nacional (National Holiday)

November 1 – Fiesta Madrileña (local festivity in Madrid)

November 1 – Todos los Santos (All Saints Day)

November 9 – Fiesta Madrileña (local festivity in Madrid)

The Statue of Columbus

December 8 – Inmaculada Concepción (day of the Immaculate Conception)

December 25 – Navidad (Christmas)

Spring and fall have many rainy days, so an umbrella is an important piece of luggage. The Madrid air is very dry because of the city's altitude, so a lip salve and moisturizer for the face are essential.

Documents

Those in possession of Western European, United States or South American passports do not need a visa. Those from other countries will need to

The Massive Edificio de España, 350 ft. high

obtain a visa from the Spanish Consulate.

There are two types of tourist visas: regular, valid for 90 days, which allows three entries and exits to and from Spain, and a tourist visa for a specified period of time not exceeding 90 days. There is a token charge, and you will receive the visa within a week from your application.

Anyone intending to drive in Spain must have an international driver's license.

Students may take advantage of reduced rates in many places, so they should have an international student's card with them.

CUSTOMS
Every tourist is allowed to enter Spain with unlimited amounts of Spanish and any other currency. On leaving, one may take up to 1,000,000 *pesetas* in Spanish currency and up to $8,000 or an equivalent amount in any other currency. If one wishes to take out more than $8,000, one must declare this in advance and receive the appropriate receipt, which should be shown on exit.

You are not allowed to enter Spain with weapons and drugs, and for items not intended for your personal use, you need a special permit.

Tourists can bring in personal effects without restriction, but will need to show receipts of payment for articles of value, such as cameras, radios and watches. One can bring in a limited amount of duty-free items, such as 400 cigarettes, 500 grams of tobacco, 2 liters of liquer, etc.

INSURANCE
It is very important to insure your property and yourself. Medical insurance when traveling abroad is a necessity, whether made through a health plan or through an insurance or travel agent. Make sure to keep all medical bills, and, if involved in an accident, keep a copy of the police report as well. Note: medical care and hospitalization are very expensive.

Budget

This depends on you! A double room in a three-star hotel is approximately $100. Meals, transport and refreshments, tours and shopping will all eat into your budget, so you just have to take what you can afford and live accordingly.

What to Wear

Once you have decided on the date of your visit, you must work out what clothes you will need. As we said, the summer is very hot, with temperatures sometimes reaching 40°C. In other words, you should pack your very lightest clothes. Ladies musn't forget to bring a headscarf for visits to churches or other holy sites. Madrid has some public and private swimming pools, and most of the hotels have pools too, so bring a swimsuit.

In winter, temperatures are around zero, so come prepared. In addition to warm clothing, bring woollen socks, gloves, and any other woollies you may have.

The inhabitants of Madrid take good care of their appearance. Men and women dress tastefully, if a little conservatively. It is usual, but not essential, to dress elegantly if you are going out in the evening. Men on business in Madrid will do well to pack at least one tie.

Picking and choosing at the Rastro Market

PART THREE – EASING THE SHOCK: WHERE HAVE WE LANDED?

Transportation

Planes, trains, automobiles and buses all go to Madrid.

FROM THE AIRPORT TO MADRID

Hundreds of flights arrive at Madrid's **Barajas Airport**, which is one of the largest in Europe. Barajas is situated about 16 kms from the city, and the most convenient way to get there is on the Barcelona highway, the NII. Approved for building in 1929, the airport's first terminal was opened two years later. Over the years, the area has become industrialized, and hotels and housing for workers have also been built there. Today the airport has four terminals (international, internal, freight, and a special terminal for irregular flights), two long runways and two shorter ones.

The airport offers varied services: cafeterias, duty-free shops, car rental offices, 24 hour banks, a telephone exchange (for international calls too), hotel reservations desk, taxi ranks and bus stations.

If you have booked a room at one of the airport hotels, the hotel will take care of your transport from and to the airport.

As in most places in the world, it is difficult to reach an understanding with the taxi drivers. You must demand that he start the fare meter at the beginning of your journey – an "all-in-one price" will not be to your advantage. On the rear window of every taxi-cab is a price list.

The bus service from the airport to the city center is convenient and cheap. The buses leave every 10 minutes, and the fare is about one dollar. The bus has an extensive luggage compartment, opened only at the start and end of the journey, which lasts between 20 and 40 minutes depending on the traffic. This is your first look at Madrid: What you see is a fairly representative cross-section – an industrial housing project near the airport, a little further on is a middle-class residential and office district, and then an old and prestigious residential area. The final stop

is at Plaza Colón, which is the very heart of the city. This service runs from 4:45am-1:15am. (Tel. 401-9900 or 431-6192 for details.)

TRAINS

There are three railway stations in Madrid: **Atocha**, which is fairly centrally situated, is frequented by trains from the south, the west and from Portugal; **Norte Príncipe Pío**, also not far from the city center, is frequented by trains from the northwest; and **Chamartín**, the biggest and most important railway station,

Only Chamartín has services of international standard: banks, stores, car rental offices, hotel reservation desks, etc. At the other stations the services are minimal: cafeterias, news agents and cigarette kiosks.

For train tickets and information, the head office of *Renfe* (the Spanish Railways Authority) is at 44 Calle Alcalá, (Metro: Banco). For information call Tel. 530-0202, for seat reservations, Tel. 527-3333.

Other *Renfe* offices are located at Plaza de España, Torre de Madrid (Tel. 542-9259), 17 Canarias (Tel. 468-4511), Barajas Airport (Tel. 305-8544) and in Chamartín, Atocha and Norte-Príncipe Pío stations.

At the Atocha Railway Station

which is located in the north of the city, is frequented by trains from the north, the east and the west, including Barcelona, Bilbao, Cádiz, Córdoba, Málaga, Santander and Seville. Trains from France arrive here as well.

Important: In recent years, the left luggage services at the airport and stations have been canceled for security reasons. However, there are three places in Madrid which still provide this service: at the airport bus terminal in the city center, under the Plaza Colón; at the inter-urban bus station Sur, next to the Palos de Moguer metro station and at the Chamartín train station.

BY ROAD

Six main highways lead to
Madrid:

NI: Irun-Madrid – road leading
north, almost as far as the
French border, passing
through Borgos, Bilbao and
San Sebastián.

NII: Barcelona-Madrid –
leading north-east, passes the
airport and through Guadala-
jara and Saragossa.

NIII: Valencia-Madrid –
leading south to the coast.
NIV: Cádiz-Madrid – passing
through Aranjuez, Cordova
and Seville.

NV: Badajoz-Madrid – leading
south-west, to the Portuguese
border.

NVI: La Coruña-Madrid –
leading north-west, towards
Galicia.

Sign-posts to help you get around

Urban Transportation

Buses: The best way to get
around in Madrid and at the
same time to enjoy the city, is
by bus. The city buses (belonging to *EMT*; *Empresa
Municipal de Transportes*) are
red, and run from 6am until
midnight. From midnight to
6am there is a limited service,
leaving Plaza de la Cibeles and
Puerta del sol on some of the
inter-city lines: until 2am, once
every half-hour, and from 2-
6am every hour. The night
service is slightly more expensive, but with free line-to-line
transfers. *Madrileños* call the
night buses "owls".

The *Bonobus* ticket, which is
valid for ten rides at a reduced
rate, can be bought at the following *EMT* stations: Cibeles,
Atocha, Moncloa, Cuatro
Caminos, Puerta del Sol,
Callao, Alcántara, Cruz de los
Caminos, Manuel Becerra and
Pio XII. General information
about the services can also be
obtained here.

In addition to the regular lines,
there is a smaller service of,
yellow buses called Microbus-
es. These are more
comfortable, but slightly more
expensive.

For general information about
bus services, Tel. 401-9900.

Metro: The metro is the
quickest way to get about. It
operates from 6am-1:30am,

except for the line to Ciudad Universitaria (7am-10pm, doesn't run on Sundays, Saturdays, holidays and throughout August). The fares are a little lower than for the buses. There is a special metro pass for tourists – *bonometro* – valid for ten days. It can be bought at the ticket offices at the entrance to the metro stations. Regular tickets can also be bought at the entrance, either at the ticket office or from automatic vending machines. You can transfer from line to line without buying another ticket.

The Madrid metro was opened in 1919, and despite numerous renovations to the old stations and trains, traveling this way is not very comfortable. There is, however, a big difference between the older city lines and those further from the center, which are more modern and smoother.

For information, Tel. 435-2266.

Taxis: There are about 15,000 taxis in Madrid. They are black or white with a red stripe on the side. The front window of an available taxi bears a sign saying "*Libre*". At night they have an illuminated green sign on the roof. Every taxi carries a tariff list. Taxi companies:

Radio Taxi: Tel. 447-5180
Radioteléfono Taxi:
Tel. 547-8200
Tele-Taxi: Tel. 445-9008.

Car Rental
Because of the traffic problems in Madrid it is not recommended to drive around, but if you do rent a car, remember:

Check your car carefully before you set out.
The local car-rental companies are cheaper than the international ones; the latter, however, are usually more reliable.

There are week-end and holiday rates.
Deposits vary from company to company. Delivery of the

car may be at the airport or at your hotel.

V.A.T. on car rental is about 15%.

The road signs on the way out of the city are clear. Madrid's rush hours are worth noting: if you want to avoid the morning rush hour, leave before 7:30am or between 9-11am. Between 4-6pm traffic moves at a fair speed and after 8:30pm it is also trouble-free. If you speak Spanish, you can get road and traffic information at Tel. 535-2222. This is especially important in winter, when many roads are closed to traffic because of the snow.

In the central areas of the city there is a parking supervision system (ORA). You have to pay for every half-hour, and the maximum parking time allowed is one-and-a-half hours. Parking tickets can be bought at any cigarette kiosk. The cards are colored as follows:

– Half hour – yellow card
– One hour – green card
– One and a half hours – pink card

There are also some municipal parking lots which you can find on the accompanying map, together with the number of parking spaces in each one.

Should you need towing or any other garage services, you should call *RACE – the Real Automóvil Club de España* – at Tel. 593-3333.

A list of car rental firms and their addresses follows:

ATESA
Aeropuerto de Barajas, Tel. 305-8660.
83 Orense, Tel. 570-4609.

AVIS
Aeropuerto de Barajas, Tel.
305-4273/4.
60 Gran Vía, Tel. 547-2048.
23 Padre Damián (*Eurobuilding* Hotel), Tel. 457-9893.
Plaza de Colón (Bus Terminal), Tel. 576-2862.
32 Agustín de Foxá, Tel. 733-3230.
AZCA Center, 22-24 Orense (*Holiday Inn* Hotel), Tel. 556-7492.

EUROPCAR
Aeropuerto de Barajas, Tel.
305-4420.
29 Orense, Tel. 555-9930.
8 San Leonardo, Tel. 541-8892

HERTZ
Aeropuerto de Barajas, Tel.
305-8452/5.
88 Gran Vía, Tel. 542-5805.
44 Doctor Fleming,
Tel. 345-1897/8/9.
Chamartín Station,
Tel. 733-0400.

ITAL
59 Alcántara, Tel. 574-6919.
18 Avenida de los Toreros, Tel. 255-4478.

Automobile Services
Ada: 19 Anastasio Herrero, Tel. 561-1255 (Madrid and vicinity); Tel. 450-1000 (rest of Spain).
Europ Assistance: 4 Orense, 1st floor, Tel. 597-2125.
General Information on Roads: Tel. 441-7222.
Mondial Assistance: 26 Modesto Lafuente, 2nd floor, Tel. 441-1866.
RACE: 10 José Abascal, Tel.

593-3333 (emergency service 24 hours a day).

Car Parks
Here is a list of car parks in Madrid:

Almagro; Plaza del Arquitecto Ribera; Plaza de Beravente; Paseo de Recoletos; Plaza del Carmen; Plaza de Colón; Plaza de las Cortes; Plaza de las Descalzas; Plaza de España; Avenida de Felipe II; Calle de Fuencarral; Luna-Judescos; Plaza del Marquis de Salamenca; Calle del Marquis de Urquijo; Plaza Major; Calle de Montalbán; Plaza de los Montenses; Plaza del Rey; Plaza de Santa Ana; Plaza de Santo Domingo; Calle de Sevilla; Plaza de Vásquez de Mella; Calle Velázquez (Ayala); Calle Velázquez (Jorge Juan); Calle Velázquez (Juan Bravo); Plaza Villa de Paria; Montevideo.

Accommodation

There is a large choice of varied accommodations at all levels in Madrid, from prestigious deluxe hotels (*Gran Lujo*), which are better than five-star hotels, to cheap *pensiones* (also called *hostales* or *residencias*) which provide basic services.

Hotels are graded according to international star ratings, and generally speaking, standards are in accordance with the ratings.

If the hotel displays a sign showing the letter "R", it indicates that the hotel has no restaurant, but guests can order breakfast, however this is not included in the price of the room. The price of a room does not always include the service of keeping valuables in the hotel safe. It is best to sort out such details when checking into a hotel.

There are many hotels, both luxurious and less expensive in the center of town. Even without advance booking, you are sure to find a room to suit your taste and budget somewhere around the Gran Vía.

If you are on a limited budget and want a cheap hotel or *pensión*, first check the cleanliness – you may find that you prefer to move on and find a cleaner place. Most of the cheap accommodation is in the area around Puerta del Sol, in the city center. In any event, avoid the hotels on Montera and Cruz streets, which are, to put it mildly, questionable. When checking in, find out what time the *pensión* closes at night, and whether the price includes use of a shower. Breakfast is never included .It is preferable, cheaper and tastier to eat elsewhere.

The following is a list of hotels, according to grade:

LUXURY HOTELS

Ritz Madrid: 5 Plaza de la Lealtad, Tel. 521-2857, Fax 532-8776. Near the Prado. Extremely luxurious, in turn of the century style.

Villa Magna: 22 Paseo de la Castellana,

Tel. 576-7500, Fax 575-9504. An excellent location right in the center of town.

5-STAR HOTELS

Husa Princesa: 40 Princesa, Tel. 542-3500, Fax 542-3501. An ultra-modern hotel. Centrally located.

Tryp Monte Real: 17 Arroyo Fresno (Puerta de Hierro), Tel. 316-2140, Fax 316-3934. With conference rooms.

Wellington: 8 Velázquez, Tel. 575-4400, Fax 576-4164. Centrally located.

4-STAR HOTELS

Palace: 7 Plaza de las Cortes, Tel. 429-7551, Fax 429-8266. This old hotel is in a beautiful, old building.

Meliá Madrid: 27 Princesa, Tel. 541-8200, Fax 541-1988. Luxurious and centrally located.

Pullman Calatrava: 1 Tutor, Tel. 541-9880, Fax 542-5736. An excellent hotel – recommended! (no dining room service).

Castellana Inter-continental: 49 Paseo de la Castellana, Tel. 410-0200, Fax 319-5853. Well located.

Emperador: 53 Gran Vía, Tel. 547-2800, Fax 547-2817. With a swimming pool.

Eurobuilding: 8 Juan Ramón Jiménez, Tel. 345-4500, Fax 345-4576. A very good hotel, especially for business people. Many international congresses are held here.

Liabeny: 3 Salud, Tel. 532-5306, Fax 532-7421. No dining room service.

Mayorazgo: 3 Flor Baja, Tel. 547-2600, Fax 541-2485. No dining room service.

Tryp Plaza: 2 Plaza de España, Tel. 547-1200, Fax 548-2389. Centrally situated with a swimming pool.

3-STAR HOTELS
Tryp Capitol: 41 Gran Vía, Tel. 521-8391, Fax 521-7729. A good hotel, well situated and convenient. No dining room service.

Gran Vía: 25 Gran Vía, Tel. 522-1121, Fax 521-2424. No dining room service.

Príncipe Pío: 14 Cuesta de San Vicente, Tel. 247-8000, Fax 541-1117.
Good location behind Plaza de España.

Puerta de Toledo: 4 Glorieta Puerta de Toledo,
Tel. 474-7100, Fax 474-0747.

Tryp Rex: 43 Gran Vía, Tel. 547-4800, Fax 547-1238. Centrally located.

2-STAR HOTELS
Alexandra: 29 San Bernardo, Tel. 542-0400, Fax 559-2825. No dining room service.

Francisco 1: 15 Arenal, Tel. 248-0204, Fax 542-2899.

PENSIÓNES WITH PRIVATE FACILITIES
Here are some good family hotels; all rooms with private bathrooms.

Astur: 64 Gran Vía, Tel. 559-4485.
Continental: 44 Gran Vía, Tel. 521-4640.
La Plata: 15 Gran Vía, Tel. 531-9737.
Breogán: 25 Fuencarral, Tel. 522-8153.

The following addresses are apartments which serve as cheap, comfortable *pensiónes*, mainly suited for students: 7 Zorilla, 44 Juan Alvarez Mendizábal.

YOUTH HOSTELS
Madrid has two good youth hostels. One is at 28 Calle

Santa Cruz de Marcenado, which can be reached by bus no. 2 from José Antonio. The other hostel is called *Richard Schirmann* on Casa de Campo, and can be reached by Metro Norte from Lago, or by bus no. 33.

For further details call Tel. 401-1300 or 455-8800, or contact the Municipal Youth Department of Madrid, which is called *Ayuntamiento de Madrid*, *Departamento de Juventud*, at 30 Paseo del Prado, Tel. 588-8341.

CAMP SITES

Information about camp sites can be obtained from the Federación Madrileña de Camping y Caravaning, 4 Santa Polonia, Madrid, Tel. 429-5223.

Practical Information

Tourist Information

When planning your trip to Spain, you can use the Spanish Tourist Information Centers situated in most major European capitals and in several cities in North America:

England: Spanish Tourist Office. 57-58 St. James's Street, London SW-1A-1LD. Tel. (071) 499-0901, Fax (071) 629-4257. Open 9am-4:30pm.

U.S.A: Tourist Office of Spain.

8383 Wilshire Boulevard, Suite 960, Beverly Hills, California 90211. Tel. (213) 658-7188, Fax (213) 658-1061. Open 9am-3pm; 665 Fifth Avenue New York, N.Y. 10022. Tel. (212) 759-8822, Fax (212) 980-1053. Open 9.30am-5.30pm; Water Tower Place, Suite 915 East 845, North Michigan Avenue, Chicago, Illinois 60-611. Tel. (312) 642-1992, Fax (312) 642-9817. Open 9am-5pm; 1221 Brickell Avenue, Miami, Florida 33131. Tel. (305) 358-1992, Fax (305) 358-8223.

Canada: Tourist Office of Spain. 102 Bloor Street west, 14th floor, Toronto, Ontario. M55 1M8. Tel (416) 961-3131, Fax (416) 961-1992. Open 9am-5pm.

Australia: Spanish National Tourist Office. Level 2 – Suite 21.A, 203 Castlereagh Street, Sydney N.S.W 2000. P.O.B. 675. Tel (02) 264-7966, Fax (02) 267-5111.

In Madrid, tourist information centers are located at the following places:

Oficina Municipal de Turismo (Municipal Tourist Information): 3 Plaza Mayor, Tel. 366-5477, 366-4874.

Dirección General de Turismo: 132 Príncipe de Vergara, Tel. 580-2441.

Barajas Airport (International Arrivals Terminal),
Tel. 305-8656.
Chamartín Railway Station, Tel. 315-9976.
2 Duque de Madinaceli, Tel. 429-4951, 315-9976.
429-4487.
Plaza de España, Torre de Madrid, Tel. 541-2325.
Turespaña – Secretaría General de Turismo:
Tel. 901-300-600 (by phone only).

Banks and Currency
The *peseta* is the Spanish currency and is an indivisible unit. One U.S. dollar is equivalent to about 145 *pesetas*. A *duro* is a 5 *peseta* coin, a *real* is a 25 *peseta* coin. The Spanish often quote prices in *duros*.

One can change foreign currency at any bank. Banking hours are Mon.-Fri. 9am-2pm and on Saturdays from 9am-12:30pm. At the airport and at the Atocha and Chamartín train stations, one can change money at any hour. In addition, the large department stores (*El Corte Inglés* and *Galerías Preciados*) have currency exchanges. At 4 and 5-star hotels and at travel agencies there is usually a department for currency exchange. Of course, one gets the best exchange rate at banks. (Changing money on the black market is inadvisable, as it is regarded as a serious offense.)

Most international credit cards are accepted in Madrid.

Opening Hours
Most shops are open from 9:30am-1pm and from 5pm-8pm. Department stores are open continuously from 10am-8pm. VIP shops, boutiques, s and restaurants, are open from 9am-3am. Restaurants generally serve meals from 1-4pm and from 8pm-midnight, but to satisfy tourists many open in the evening before 8pm.

Purchase Tax
In department stores you can claim a 7.2% return on purchases over $400. Just ask the shop for a three-copied tax form, fill in your purchases and what you paid and give the forms to customs when you leave.

They will send your 7.2% to the address on the form. There are some shops, though not many, who will deduct the tax when you pay.

Tipping

Here are a few guidelines: Service is included at hotels and restaurants, but it is customary to add 10% for waiters; taxi drivers should get 5-10% of the fare; hairdressers 10%; chambermaids get about 150 *pesetas*. Porters' rates are displayed.

Language and Manners

If you need to ask for assistance, take into account that although the average *Madrileño* does not know many languages, he will go out of his way to help you, using a polite torrent of words and an unlimited range of gestures. A handshake is customary between new male acquaintances, while the women usually kiss. The younger generation tend to greet one another with a kiss regardless of sex. The morning greeting is *Buenos días*; afternoon – *Buenas tardes*, and on retiring for the night – *Buenas noches*. If those are difficult to remember, you can always say *Hóla* when you arrive, and *Adiós* when you leave. It is customary to speak a word of greeting on entering a shop, and when leaving a bar or restaurant. At the end of this guide you will find a short glossary which includes some useful words you may need during your visit.

The bars – it must be mentioned that if you are fanatically clean, you'd better keep your eyes closed. Patrons are accustomed to throwing paper napkins, cigarette butts, olive pits, etc. under the table. A waiter will sweep up every now and then, but his efforts often prove futile. Ashtrays and trash-cans have appeared in some places recently, but these are the exception rather than the rule.

Keeping in Touch

It is cheaper to make phone calls from post offices rather than hotels. There are three main exchanges in Madrid:

The central post office at the Plaza de la Cibeles. Open from 8am-1pm.

The Telephone Company building at 3 Fuencarral. Open from 9am-10pm, and on Sundays and holidays from 10am-2pm and 5-9pm.

The Exchange, at 10 Virgen de los Peligros. Open from 9am-1pm and 5-9pm, and on Sundays and holidays from 10am-3pm.

The area code of Madrid is 91, 1 only if calling from abroad.

TELEX AND FAX

Telex and fax services are available at the Central Post Office from 8am-midnight. You can also receive telexes and faxes provided you set the date and time with the sender. For information, Tel. 5218195, or ask at the airport.

POST OFFICE

Post offices are open from 9am-1pm and 5pm-7pm.

Poste Restante (in Spanish: *Lista de Correos*) service is available at the Central Post Office (Plaza de la Cibeles), between 9am-10pm.

Postage stamps are available at cigarette kiosks which are called *estancos*, as well as at all post offices.

Personal Security

Madrid was once considered a fairly safe city, but over the past few years muggings have increased, and you should take precautions. The most risky places are the *Rastro* (the Sunday market) and anywhere where there are crowds. Madrid's thieves are nimble bag-snatchers and pickpockets. There is no need for panic, but you should be careful. Despite this, you may walk safely in the streets at any time of night or day. Any case of theft should be reported at the nearest police station. Be sure to get a police report – usually necessary for insurance claims.

Health

For urgent medical care you can refer to the following hospitals:

La Paz: 261 Paseo de la Castellana, Tel. 358-0851.
Palacio 8: 147 Extremadura, Tel. 464-7632.
Centro: 10 Navas de Tolosa, Tel. 521-0025, 522-3191. Near Plaza del Callao.
Retiro: 39 Gobernador, Tel. 420-0356. Near Paseo del Prado.
Tetuan Chamartín: 357 Bravo Murillo. Tel. 579-1223.
Universidad: 1 Vallehermoso, Tel. 446-2675.

Measurements, Electricity and Time

Measurements: The metric system is in use in Spain – weight is in kilograms, clothing and shoe sizes go according to the European system. Below is a conversion table which may be useful.

WEIGHT

25 grams – 1 ounce
453 grams – 1 pound

1 kilogram – 2.2 pounds

VOLUME
0.47 liters – 1 pint
1 liter – approximately 1 quart
3.79 liters – 1 gallon

DISTANCE
2.4 centimeters – 1 inch
30.5 centimeters – 1 foot
1 meter – approximately 1 yard

1 kilometer – 0.628 miles
1.6 kilometers – 1 mile

Electric current is usually 220v. In the older districts there are some places which still use 125v, so be sure to ask.

Time in Spain is GMT+1, through the summer, from the beginning of April clocks are put forward one hour.

MADRID

MADRID – AREA BY AREA

Ancient Madrid

Metro: Sol, Lines 1, 2, and 3.
Buses: 5, 15, 17, 20, 23, 50, 51, 52, and 53.

This tour will lead us among streets and buildings which have existed since the time the Hapsburg dynasty ruled Spain in the 16th century. Madrid had recently been declared the new capital by Philip II, and the kings began to build and add splendor to the city. Nevertheless, the town retained its original character, and continued to function as a meeting-place for the farmers of the area, who used to sell their produce here. Large numbers of servants, craftsmen and functionaries gathered at court, busy with their intrigues and gossip.

Our tour begins in the main square – Plaza Mayor. Entering the square, we step into another era. On weekdays, the atmosphere here is peaceful, and the gray stone buildings which enclose the square create an area which is entirely different from its surroundings. When first built, the square served as a market-place for fish, meat, bread and water, and was surrounded by modest houses and shops. At the end of the 16th century these houses and shops were pulled down and the two principal buildings in the

The statue of King Philip III at Plaza Mayor

square were built: Casa de la Panadería (bakery) and Casa de la Carnicería (butcher). When the royal court moved to Madrid, some futile attempts were made to enhance the square. In 1617, work was begun which was to last for two years during the reign of Philip III.

In the 19th century the Plaza Mayor attained the pinnacle of its greatness, playing host to all the city's great events: coronations, tournaments, bullfights, religious ceremonies and even executions, which were then something of a spectator sport. The first event to

Hundreds of years old, ornate architecture in Plaza Mayor

be celebrated here was the sanctification of Isidro, patron saint of Madrid, on May 15, 1620. To this day, celebrations in his honor still begin here, opened by the mayor, with artists and crowds filling the square to capacity. Years ago, the houses had wooden balconies, from which the court entourage would view the many happenings. Fires, however, destroyed the wooden structures surrounding the square time after time, and in 1791 the architect Juan de Villanueva ordered that the pillars around the square, the balconies and the roofed entrances be built of stone. Since then no changes have been made except for the addition of the statue of Philip III, which was erected in 1847. Some years ago, when the statue was being restored, a "graveyard" of birds was discovered in the belly of the horse – the poor creatures had entered via the horse's open mouth and had been unable to find their way out again. The mouth has now been blocked up.

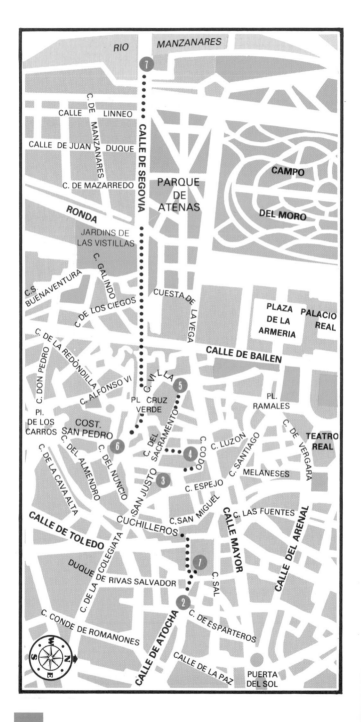

In spring and summer, music, dancing and theatrical shows are held in the square, and on Sundays, throughout the year, there is a stamp and coin fair. On the days preceding Christmas, this is the place to buy Christmas trees and colorful decorations. The square is at its most beautiful in the quiet early hours of the morning, when you can sit at one of the tables and enjoy the the wintry sun or the cool summer shade, while sipping a cup of steaming coffee and looking around. You can almost forget the reality of time, which seems to stand still here.

Taking a break from the bustle of the city at Plaza Mayor

We leave the square via the Gerona Gate and walk right into the small and noisy **Plaza de la Provincia** (Province Square). Opposite, we can see an impressive building – **Palacio de Santa Cruz**, today housing the Ministry of Foreign Affairs. Built during the reign of Philip IV as a prison, the façade was originally adorned with an angel, and there was a popular saying – "To sleep under the wings of the angel"– which meant to be a "guest" at the institution. Indeed, many and important people have slept under the wings of that angel, such as the great dramatist Lope de Vega, who was constantly in trouble over women, and Luis Candelas, a kind of Madrid Robin Hood, who used to rob the rich in the city's squares, and became a legend in local folklore. The building is one of the finest examples of the architecture of the Hapsburg dynasty, a style which combined stone, red brick and slate roofs.

The 18th century Basílica de San Miguel

We return to the Plaza Mayor and leave it via the "Escalinata de Piedra" ("Stone Steps"). It is said that this is the very spot where Luis Candelas was executed, and a lovely inn now stands there in his memory. We go out to Calle de Cuchilleros (Street of the Knifers), which owes its name not, as might be supposed, to bloody knife battles, but to the peace-loving craftsmen who worked their metals here. Looking back from the bottom of the steps, to the left we can see Calle Cava de San Miguel. The word *cava* is an Arabic word which describes the under-ground passageways built by the Moslems to serve for surprise attacks, or for retreats in times of difficulty. Nothing remains of the street's war-ridden Moslem history. Its charming appearance dates back to the early 19th century, when the poorest of Madrid's citizens lived here – those who flourished in the wonderful stories *Fortunata y Jacinta* by Benito Perez Galdos.

Calle de Cuchilleros – the "Street of the Knifers"

Back on Calle de Cuchilleros, there is a colorful array of eating places and work-shops. Close to the stone steps, above the *Arco de Cuchilleros* restaurant, a sign announces "Hemingway never ate here" – in direct contrast to the many signs to be seen at the entrances to other places, which would have you believe that the writer patronized them regular-ly. If they are all true, it's a bit difficult to understand when he found time to write... A little further on is one of the city's oldest restaurants, *Sobrinos del*

Botín, founded in 1725 and specializing in meat dishes. At the end of the street we can see the modern murals which add color, if not elegance, to the **Plaza de la Puerta Cerrada** (Square of the Locked Door). This name recalls the fact that this was once the site of the city wall, and just here there was a door, which was locked at night against bandits and wild animals. In those days, Madrid was still surrounded by forests inhabited by wild boar, bears and wolves. On one of the murals a sign reads "I was built on water and my walls are fire". Years ago people used to ask the riddle: "Which city is built on water, surrounded by fire, has cats for citizens, and is entered through a locked door?" The answer was, of course, Madrid, the explanation being that the city is built on ground water, its walls were built of flint (firestone), the *Madrileños* were once nicknamed *gatos* (cats), and the locked door we have already mentioned. Today, the only place worth a visit in this square is the *Casa Paco* – a very old restaurant and café serving excellent meat dishes and local wines.

Grace, Valor, Faith and Hope – the four statuettes afront Basílica de San Miguel

We now continue along Calle San Justo as far as the **Basílica de San Miguel**. This lovely 18th century church is a fine example of Italian baroque style. The façade is adorned with statues of four allegorical figures: "Grace" and "Valor" below, and "Faith" and "Hope" above. Above the main altar there is a painting by Alejandro Ferrant depicting the archangel Michael, battling the rebellious angels.

Turning right into Calle Puñon-rostro, we are close to the palace of the Puñonrostro family. The name literally means "a punch in the face". The name was appar-ently acquired because the founder of the family used to deliver blows to the faces of the enemies of King Carlos I. In

appreciation of those blows, he was made a Count!

Further on, we turn into Calle del Codo (Elbow), which bends as its name suggests, and leads us to the Plaza de la Villa (Town Square). This elegant and peaceful square is surrounded by harmoniously integrated buildings, even though each of them is a memento of a different period. Looking over all this is the statue of Alvaro de Bazán, hero of the battle of Lepanto (the battle at which Cervantes, creator of Don Quixote, lost his arm). To our left is the Torre de los Lujanes (Lujanes Tower). Built in Moorish style, it is one of the few relics of 15th century architecture. The French King Francis I was incarcerated here, after daring to wage war against the Holy Roman Emperor Charles V. Next to the tower is the municipal archives building.

Hemeroteca Municipal (The Municipal Archives) is opposite the Casa de la Villa (Town Hall). It is a small building, built in Arab-influenced Mudéjar style. At the entrance are the graves of Beatriz Galindo and her husband. Beatriz, known as "La Latina", was Latin teacher to the Catholic Queen Isabel, and was an extremely interesting person. Her wisdom was a byword at the royal court; people would say of her that "everything goes into her head". She was the queen's permanent advisor and companion, and also served as tutor to her children. Together with her husband, she built a hospital and charitable institutions. Madrid expressed its admiration and

Torre de los Lujanes – a relic of 15th century architecture

appreciation by naming one of the town's districts after her. The hospital built by "La Latina" has since been destroyed, but its Gothic balustrade was transfered to the archives building.

The statue of Aluard de Bazán, hero of the battle of Lepanto, at Plaza de la Villa

Opposite us now we can see the **Casa de la Villa** (Town Hall). When Madrid became the capital, a town hall was needed which would suit municipal needs and also enhance the town's stature. The architect Gomez de Mora (who also built the Santa Cruz Palace), planned this building in the 17th century. In 1787, Juan de Villanueva added the balcony overlooking the Calle Mayor, where the kings would sit to watch religious processions. The combination of stone and red brick with slate roofs had become the main feature of the town's architecture. Life in Madrid was run from this building, and opposite the citizens of the town would assemble to cheer or protest. By the beginning of this century, the building was too small to encompass the extensive activities of the growing city, and the municipality purchased the nearby **Casa de Cisneros** (Cisneros House). This fine building was built in the second half of the 17th century, in the Plateresque style. The house is named for Bishop Cisneros (1436-1517), who ruled in Spain after the death of the Catholic Fernando. He founded the *Alcalá de Herares University*, financed the translation of the Bible into Spanish – but never actually lived in this palace. Both these municipal buildings may be visited on Mon. at 5pm. For additional details, Tel. 542-5512, 548-7426.

Casa de Cisneros faces Calle Sacramento, which we reach by going along Calle Cordón (Shoelace). The poet Emilio Carrera wrote of Calle Sacramento:

The tower of Iglesia de San Pedro

> *Sacramento Street*
> *Dozing in ancient charm*
> *Old castles*
> *Noble palaces*
> *Pleasant corners*
> *Where dreams are so sweet...*

Unfortunately, little remains of the "ancient charm" of the street except the façade of Casa de Cisneros and a 19th century church, **Iglesia de las Bernardas**, at the end of the street, whose external simplicity includes a relief glorifying the saints Benito and Bernard.

From here we go to the end of a small street called Calle de los Consejos, and we continue along Calle de la Villa, until we reach **Plaza de la Cruz Verde** (Square of the Green Cross). The fountain in this charming square was built in 1850, and is dedicated to Diana, goddess of the hunt. The romantic aura of the square allows us to almost forget that here the Inquisition used to hold its benighted ceremonies. At these ceremonies – *autos-da-fé* – at which citizens were forced to repent their alleged actions, religious plays were performed, public sermons were delivered and sentences were pronounced and carried out on "sinners" and "heretics".

We now ascend the steps which lead to a tiny square – **Plaza de San Janvier**. There are several small squares in this area which were much-loved by the Moslems who once lived here. We cross the busy Calle de Segovia and go left until Calle Costanilla de San Pedro, where we find the **Iglesia de San Pedro** (Church of San Pedro). Many tales have been told of the bells which hang in the *Mudéjar*-style tower here. It is said that when the bells were brought to the foot of the tower it became clear that they were too big to be carried up the staircase. Many attempts were made, all in vain. The defeated workmen went back to their homes, and when they returned, despondently the following morning, to their astonishment they found the bells in their appointed place. And that's not all! It is also said that these bells had the power to prevent hail, and the farmers would ask that the bells be rung whenever there were threatening clouds in the sky. These bells would ring without human interference whenever tragedies occurred in the city (such as the death of Philip II, the French

In the dark days of the Inquisition autos-da-fé were held at Plaza de la Cruz Verde

The Viaducto – planned in the 18th century but completed only in 1931

invasion, or the many epidemics which afflicted the city). The building itself, simple and somewhat rustic, is a fine memorial to the Madrid of years ago.

We return to Calle Segovia and turn left, walking west. Several streets further on we pass beneath the Viaducto (see "The Western Districts"). The **Parque de las Vistillas** (Vistillas Park) is to one side; a green expanse covering the steep slope leading to the top of the hill. We carry on as far as the **Segovia Bridge,** with the green park to our right and a quiet residential district to our left. This monumental bridge was the first attempt to bestow on Madrid the grand entrance befitting a capital city. King Philip II appointed architect Juan de Herrera for the project, and the result, impressive though it may be, is particularly notable for the lack of proportion between the structure itself and the trickle of water beneath it, masquerading as a river.

To the Palace!

Buses: Circular, 25, 33, 36, 41, 50.

From the 16th century, we progress geographically, chronological-
ly and status-wise to royalty. The gardens and buildings along this
route comprise an impressive and elegant collection, befitting the
very heart of the kingdom.

We begin this tour at the Segovia Bridge,
and take a pleasant stroll along the **Paseo de
la Virgen Puerto** (Virgin of the Port Promenade). This lovely promenade is not given
the publicity it deserves despite its beauty.
To the right stretch the **Parque de Atenas**
(Athens Park) and **Campo del Moro**
(Garden of the Moor), and to the left the
meandering Mensanares River. We walk
first along the left side, where the municipal
tennis courts separate the street from the
Mensanares, until we reach the **Ermita de
la Virgen del Puerto**, a sanctuary built in
1718 by architect Pedro de Ribera. *Ermita* is
Spanish for hermitage and, indeed when it
was built, this district was outside the city
limits, and on festival days the citizens of
Madrid would come to picnic here, on the
banks of the Mensanares. Crossing the road,
we enter the **Campo del Moro**, a charming
corner full of greenery. What used to be the

MADRID

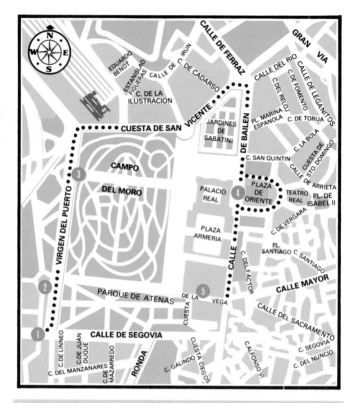

TO THE PALACE
1. Segovia Bridge
2. Ermita de la Virgen del Puerto
3. Campo del Moro
4. Palacio Real de Oriente
5. La Almudena

palace plant nurseries is now the **Museo de Carruajes** (Carriage Museum). The museum displays the old carriages of varying antiquity, used by the Spanish aristocracy. Open Mon.-Sat. 9am-6pm, Sun. and holidays 9am-3pm. Tel. 548-7404. Entrance fee.

To reach the **Palacio Real de Oriente** (Eastern Royal Palace) return to Calle Virgen del Puerto and continue until Cuesta de San Vicente, and turn right. We go up the *Cuesta* (Slope), an effort made worthwhile when we reach *Calle Bailén*, named in memory of the Battle of Bailén, one of the

84

important battles of the Spanish War of Independence against France in 1808. Open summer – Mon.-Sat. 9:am-6:15pm, Sun. and holidays 9am-2:15pm, winter – Mon.-Sat. 9am-5:15pm. Closed on offical reception days. Visits in groups and with guides. The entrance is through the right hand door of the three doors facing Plaza de Armería. Tel. 542-0059.

Turn right and look down on the beautifully landscaped **Jardines de Sabatini** (Sabatini Gardens), named after one of the palace architects. The gardens were landscaped in the 20th

The lovely Jardines de Sabatini

century and complete the lovely framework around the palace: Campo del Moro to the west, the Jardines de Sabatini to the north, and the Plaza de Oriente (Eastern Square) to the east.

The palace is on the site of the Alcázar fortress, built on this hill by the Emir Muhammad I. When Madrid became a Christian city, Alcázar was totally renovated and changed, retaining only its original shape, but then, in 1738, Alcázar and all the treasures it contained were burnt to the ground. Fortunately, at the time, the royal family was staying in the Buen Retiro Palace (see "Arts and Sciences – From Plaza de Lavapiés to the Botanical Gardens").

Palacio Real de Oriente – classical lines and white stone

Philip V wanted to build, on this spot, a palace more suited to the tastes of the time and the needs of the kingdom. The first plan was rejected, since it demanded removal to another site. Alcázar's location, on the crest of the hill, limited the size of the building. The architect Sacchetti put forward a design in which

The Throne Room at the palace – note the lavish use of gold brought in from the colonies

In the palace there are marvellously painted ceilings, designed to glorify the crown

height would compensate for this limitation. Sacchetti's work was continued by Ventura Rodríguez, who was considered to be the greatest of Madrid's architects, and by Sabatini, an Italian. Construction of the palace continued into the reign of Carlos III, successor of Philip V.

The height of the palace, its classical lines and shining white stone all help to lighten the weightiness of the huge edifice. Under the bright skies of Madrid, the palace blends impressively with its surroundings. Its physical greatness was meant to symbolize the greatness of the monarchy and the glory of the kingdom. King Carlos III succeeded in gathering around him the greatest artists of the time, most of whom were of Italian descent. In addition to the architects mentioned earlier, his court was enhanced by such artists as Conrado Giaquinto, Giovanni Battista Tiepolo, the Czech Anton Raphael Mengs, and musicians such as Luigi Bocherini and Domenico Scarlatti. Carlos III was nicknamed "The Mayor King", because of his considerable contribution to the beauty and character of Madrid.

There is an interesting anecdote about the building of the palace. When the construction work was nearing completion, the king ordered a series of statues, to be erected on the upper balustrade of the palace. They were statues of all the kings of Spain, from Atawolf (a Visigoth king) to Fernando VI. The statues were extremely heavy, and Isabella de Francio, the beautiful Italian queen who was a dominant personality and deeply superstitious, repeatedly dreamt of the statues falling on her head. Whether the original plan was changed due to the royal nightmares or for some other reason, we do not know today, but the statues were not placed on the balustrade, but rather around the Plaza de Oriente. Today the palace is no longer the royal residence, although it is used for receptions for high-ranking visitors. Open Mon.-Sat. 9am-6pm, Sun. and holidays 9am-3pm. Closed on reception days. Tel. 548-7404.

The southern wing has always been considered the main wing. Great attention was lavished on its adornment, as it contained the halls intended for official receptions. All the halls were built in the same style, expressing the dominant taste at the time of Carlos III and Carlos IV. The ceilings were painted by Giovanni Battista Tiepolo, Conrado Giaquinto and Anton Raphael Mengs. The subjects chosen were also intended to glorify the crown and the colonies. The most impressive hall is undoubtedly the Throne Room, the ceiling of which was painted by the great Tiepolo. There are also two series of bronze statues in this room – The Virtues and The Planets – and two copies of Italian statues brought to Spain by Velázquez. In the nearby Official Hall there is a painting of the fable The Power and the Greatness of the Kingdom of Spain. The paintings in the Salón de Alabarderos (Spearholders' Hall) were dedicated to The Deification of Aeneas. Giaquinto painted the domes above the main staircase and in the Hall of Pillars. Tapestries, oil-paintings and furniture complete the spectacular design of the halls. Especially noteworthy is Salón de Gasparini (Gasparini's Hall), which is decorated

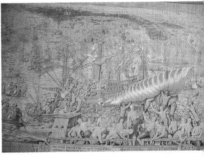

A tapestry in the palace, depicting scenes from Spain's nautical history

entirely in porcelain and embroidered silk in Chinese style. Designed by the Neapolitan artist Gasparini, the combination is a fine example of rococo style. Another example of rococo can be seen in the Sala de Porcelana (Porcelain Room).

The corner rooms have been arranged according to schools of art, and contain the paintings which used to hang in the private apartment of the royal family. The collection includes early Flemish works, 16th and 17th century Italian paintings, works by Velázquez, Goya, Rubens and others. The eastern wing houses the rooms of queen María Christina, decorated in 19th-century style, the neo-classical Hall of Mirrors and the Tapestry Hall.

Palacio Real de Oriente and Jardines de Sabatini

Outside the palace, in the **Plaza de la Armería**, we can see the Mensanares riverbed and the Guadarama Mountains. This panoramic view brings home the strategic importance of this location, and explains the wise decision of Emir Muhammad I in choosing this site to build his fortress.

Real Armería (The Royal Museum of Weapons) is situated in this square. Among the exhibits are the swords of El Cid (the

Spanish national hero), of Boadbil (the last Moslem king), of Hernán Cortés (conqueror of Mexico) and of the Catholic kings. There are also suits of armor worn by the kings of Spain, and other items of ancient weaponry.

Close by is the **Real Oficina de Farmacia** (Royal Office of Pharmacy). Here you can see ancient pharmaceutical utensils and medicines of times gone by, all of unfamiliar shapes and names.

Ancient swords and armor – at the Real Armería

Our next destination is **La Almudena**, which, fittingly enough, has a sad and royal story attached to it. It is 1878, the young King Alfonso XII married the beautiful Mercedes and all Madrid loved her and sang her praises. But this happiness did not last for long. It became known that the queen had tuberculosis, and the Madrileños thronged to the *Iglesia de la Paloma* (Church of the Dove) to ask the saint to intercede on her behalf and save her life. But their prayers went unanswered, and the young queen died a mere six months later. The grief-stricken king isolated himself, and the children of Madrid could be heard singing in the squares:

Ready for battle – at the Real Armería, situated at Plaza de la Armería

The lanterns of the king's palace
No longer shed their light
For Mercedes is dead
And they are darkened in mourning

Where will you go, Alfonso
In your grief, where will you go?
I am searching for Mercedes
It is so long since I saw her

Your Mercedes is dead
I myself saw her die
Four dukes carried her
Through the streets of Madrid.

The grave decor of La Almudena is consistent with the sad legends connected with this church

The church of La Almudena – an interesting contrast of bare walls and ornamented statues

Since the queen died childless, she could not be buried in the royal pantheon at the palace-monastery El Escorial. Alfonso decided to erect a magnificent mausoleum in the cathedral near La Almudena Palace, but his plan was never realized.

The church of La Almudena is associated with numerous legends: on November 9, 1083, when the Moslems and the Christians were still at war with each other, a section of the Moslem wall collapsed, and a wooden image of Mary with the baby Jesus was discovered. In the same niche there were said to be two candles alight, whose flame had been burning for 300 years! It was assumed that a faithful Christian had hidden the image of the Virgin when the Moslem forces had approached his village. Another version of the story tells that at the time the Christian soldiers were in despair because of their hunger, and they found a store full of wheat behind the image which saved them, by giving them the strength to complete the conquest. The Almudena Virgin, dark-skinned and lovely, is the patron saint of Madrid.

By 1518 Carlos I was thinking of building a cathedral, but the Bishop of Toledo, jealous

of the growing importance of Madrid, objected to the plan, and it was only in 1880 that a plan was finally accepted to build a neo-Gothic cathedral. In 1944, however, it was decided that it was unsuited to its surroundings and should be changed. Thus, even today the cathedral stands, without a roof, and one can see only the main façade and visit the lower hall. It is in this hall, above the main altar, that the Almudena Virgin stands.

We come out of La Almudena straight into the **Plaza de Oriente** (Eastern Square). Madrid owes this expansive square, like many others, to the French King Joseph Bonaparte, brother of Napoleon. The citizens of Madrid truly hated Joseph, who was for them the symbol and representative of conquest. They made no secret of their feelings, and their fertile imagination saw him as ugly, hunch-backed and short-sighted (which he wasn't), and as an adulterer. But Joseph Bonaparte loved Madrid and treated it well, as can be seen from the open spaces he created among the crowded buildings. However, the *Madrileños* never forgave him for his cruel repression of the rebellion which took place here on May 1, 1808.

The elegant café de Oriente offers a "get together" with true Madrileños

On that fateful morning a carriage left the palace, taking the Queen and the Princess into exile. A passing tradesman saw what was happening, and began shouting to all the passers-by – "Treason! They're taking our royal family away! Death to the French!" Thus, the rebellion was started, and it spread like wildfire throughout the city. They fought fiercely against the French forces – simple townspeople, women, children against soldiers. But the uprising was cruelly suppressed, and on May 3, many of the leaders were executed around the city. Goya commemorated the tragic events in his powerful painting *The Third of May, 1808*. Joseph Bonaparte's rule was a short one, and he managed only to demolish buildings to open space for the squares he created in the city, gaining for himself the nickname of "King of the Plazas".

Work on the Plaza de Oriente began during the reign of Fernando VII, but was completed only during that of Isabel II. A statue of Philip IV stands in the center of the square, inspired by Velázquez's wonderful painting. After walking around, you can stop for some coffee at the lovely and elegant *Café de Oriente*, in the company of the city's beautiful people.

The façade of Palacio Real de Oriente, exemplifies monarchic strength and self-assurance

The Western Districts

Metro: Opera, Lines 2, 5.
Buses: 25, 33, 39.

With the Palace and La Almudena now behind us, we are on the **El Viaducto** (Viaducto Bridge), built to span the considerable differences of height between Calle Segovia and Calle Bailén. The bridge was already planned in the 18th century, but its final construction in its present form was completed only in 1931. The view towards the Guadarrama Mountains, which can be seen clearly on fine days, includes the Casa de Campo and the Mensanares Valley.

In the other direction (eastwards) we can see Madrid, which from here looks like a mosaic of black and red roofs, white and gray walls and colorful laundry. On the eastern slope of the palace hill, is the Arab district, the *Morería*; and to the south-west, is the Jewish quarter. Crossing the bridge, we see to our right the **Parque de la Vistillas** (Vistillas Gardens) the beginning of which we saw below on Calle Segovia (see "Ancient Madrid"). In fine weather tables and garden chairs are put out and the place is packed with people: foot weary tourists taking in the scenery, townspeople basking in the sun, music and drama students from the nearby academy gossiping about the teachers and one another. We walk down to

The entrance to the Vistillas Gardens

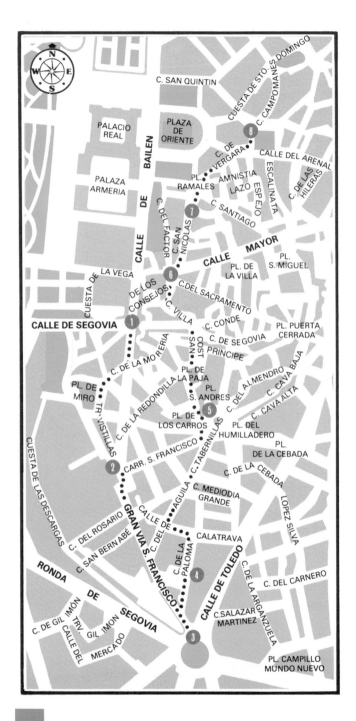

the first street and continue alongside the quiet Plaza Miro as far as Travesia Vistillas, which leads us directly to the square of the **Iglesia de San Francisco El Grande** (Church of St. Francis the Great.) According to tradition, this church was founded by St. Francis of Assisi in the 13th century. He chose this spot for its rural atmosphere and remoteness from the town, which was appropriate to his ascetic beliefs.

However, strange are the ways of the world, and the town developed in that very direction, and the Franciscan order became wealthy; and instead of communing with nature and the poor, the order became associated with the aristocracy and the leaders of the times. As a result, the original modest building was not big enough to hold all those wishing to pray, marry or be buried there, and in 1784 Sabatini, the architect of the palace, built the impressive edifice which we see today.

Inside the church, which has been undergoing renovations for the past 70 years, there is a painting by Goya, *St. Bernardino*. On the left, and in the hall of holy vessels there are 18th and 19th century paintings and carved wooden choir chairs. (Open to visitors: winter – Tues.-Sat. 11am-1pm, 5-8pm, summer – 11am-1pm, 5-8pm. Entrance fee. Tel. 565-3800.

From the church square we carry on along Calle Gran Vía de San Francisco to **Puerta**

THE WESTERN DISTRICTS
1. El Viaducto
2. Iglesia de San Francisco el Grande
3. Puerta de Toledo
4. Iglesia de la Paloma
5. Iglesia de San Andrés
6. Palacio de Uceda
7. Iglesia de San Nicolás de los Servitas
8. Plaza de Isabell II

de Toledo (Gate of Toledo). This gate was planned during the short reign of Joseph Bonaparte and was intended to glorify the French victory. But history played its own joke, and the gate was actually built in 1827, to celebrate the Spanish victory over the French.

The atmosphere changes completely now as we walk along Calle de la Paloma (Dove Street) to the **Iglesia de la Paloma** (Church of the Dove), so close to the hearts of the *Madrileños*. The dove which gave its name to the church, the street and, in fact, to the whole district, has in its origins a wondrous legend: it is told that once, during the Festival of the Holy Virgin, a persistent dove accompanied the procession along the entire route. It was learned that the dove came from a monastery where another image of the Virgin was found neglected

Puerta de Toledo – built to glorify Bonaparte's triumph, but ironically became a monument to the Spanish victory over the French

among piles of wood. To commemorate this event, the church was built in 1791. Every August the district honors the Virgin and the dove with a colorful procession of traditionally dressed *Madrileños*. There are games and lots of food and drink – recommended!

The church is not especially impressive. Over the altar hangs a picture of the Virgin with the dove flying above.

A little further along Calle de la Paloma we turn left into Calle Calatrava, and then right at the first corner, at Calle Aguila which becomes Calle Tabernillas further along. This is a working-class district remarkable for its small balconies, black iron railings and abundant flower boxes with the dominant red of geraniums. We now reach **Plaza de Carros** (Square of the Carts). This is an example of intelligent yet unsophisticated urbanization, which considers the residents and has refrained from merely trying to make an impression. It is quiet, new, small and simple, and its only decoration the outer wall of the **Iglesia de San Andrés** (San Andrés Church). Here the old people sit relaxing, watching the children at play, dogs running about and the doves flying above – a peaceful little area in the heart of the rowdy city.

The peaceful Plaza de Carros, adorned with the red-bricked San Andrés Church

Plaza de Carros is part of a system of small squares which once served the farmers of the area, who would come here to sell their produce. To the right is Plaza San Andrés and the entrance to the Iglesia de San Andrés – a fine 17th century baroque building.

We return to the Plaza de Carros and walk round the church until we reach the **Plaza de la Paja** (Square of Straw), where there are two ruined buildings: the **Palacio de Vargas** (palace of the Vargas family) and the **Capilla del Obispo** (Bishop's Chapel), both dating from the 16th century. The chapel was built as the burial place of St. Isidro. This square, which is used by the children of the nearby school as their playground, was once an important place. All that remains today are the two buildings and

The altar in the Church of the Dove

some expensive and prestigious restaurants, such as *Gure Etxea* which serves superb Basque cuisine.

We leave the square via the steep Calle Costanilla de San Andrés, and stop where it meets Príncipe Lane. From here we can see the magnificent steeple of the Iglesia de San Pedro. We now cross Calle Segovia and the Plaza de la Cruz Verde (Square of the Green Cross), and go up along Calle Costanilla Pretil Consejos to Calle Mayor. To the left of this street is the **Palacio de Uceda** (Uceda Palace), which today serves as Army Headquarters. It was designed by Gomez de Mora, the architect of the Town Hall and Plaza Mayor. This building, with its clean, simple lines, was built at the beginning of the 17th century. On the opposite sidewalk – and in contrast to the severe façade of the Palacio de Uceda – the charming **Palacio de Abrantes** (Abrantes Palace) is a most pleasant sight. This is now the Italian Embassy, and was built in 1844.

Crossing Calle Mayor, we enter the narrow Calle San Nicolás. Where this meets Calle

The Viaducto – spanning the differences of height between Calle Segovia and Calle Bailén

Cruzada, we find the **Iglesia de San Nicolás de los Servitas** (Church of San Nicolás de los Servitas), whose steeple has a few remnants of Arabic engraving. The church, which was apparently built over a mosque in the 15th century, has both Arab Mudéjar and Gothic elements. We walk on along this street as far as Plaza Ramales, with its lovely 18th century Casa de Trespalacios.

Walk along Calle Vergara, until we come directly to **Plaza de Isabel II**. This square was built at the end of the last century, and the Queen's statue stands at its center. Isabel II is remembered by the *Madrileños* in connection with wat-

er. During her reign water was brought from the Guaderama Mountains via a canal which was named in her honor. Isabel's name is engraved on the iron lids of the main pipeline at every corner in the city. There is one anecdote on the subject which tells that when the canal was opened, an astute trades-man opened a shop for the sale of shirts, foreseeing that the townspeople would now wash and change these garments more often. According to the story, the man indeed made his fortune.

The focal point of the square is regularly the **Teatro Real** (Royal Theater), or *La Opera* as the locals call it. At the moment the theater is closed for renovations. Where the theater now stands the city launderesses used to work and there was a small theater owned by a troupe of Italian singers. In 1817, during the reign of Isabel II, both the laundries and the theater were pulled down and the new theater was built. The theater opened in 1850, on Isabel's birthday, and the complex became known as "The Courtyard of Miracles". There were two seamstresses

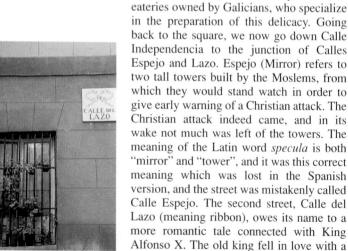

Parque de la Vistillas – on fine days tables and garden chairs are put out

who took care of the clothes of the ladies down to the last detail, a flower shop, a café, etc. During its first years, mostly Verdi operas were staged, and throughout Madrid you could hear enthusiastic, though perhaps off-key, renditions of "La Donna e Mobile!" (The Lady is Fickle). In 1870, Wagner took the audience by storm with the first operas of his *Der Ring des Nibelungun*. In the early years of this century, Diaghilev and Nijinsky arrived, bringing with them their new approaches to ballet. After World War II, the theater was closed for renovations, and reopened in 1960 as a concert hall.

To the left of the square, along Calle Escali-nata, we can try some octopus at two eateries owned by Galicians, who specialize in the preparation of this delicacy. Going back to the square, we now go down Calle Independencia to the junction of Calles Espejo and Lazo. Espejo (Mirror) refers to two tall towers built by the Moslems, from which they would stand watch in order to give early warning of a Christian attack. The Christian attack indeed came, and in its wake not much was left of the towers. The meaning of the Latin word *specula* is both "mirror" and "tower", and it was this correct meaning which was lost in the Spanish version, and the street was mistakenly called Calle Espejo. The second street, Calle del Lazo (meaning ribbon), owes its name to a more romantic tale connected with King Alfonso X. The old king fell in love with a beautiful young girl from Calle Espejo, and made her a gift of a ribbon for her hair. The girl, however, already had a young lover and the jealous king ordered that a guard watch her house. One night, in a narrow lane near Calle Espejo, the guard saw the young lover walking with the king's ribbon on his hat. The king's servants stabbed the young man in the back, and his body was left lying in that nameless alley, the ribbon stained with his blood. And so the little lane was given its name.

Now we turn right into Calle Amnistía. Here, on the corner of Calle Santa Clara, once lived the brilliant 19th-century journalist and sharp critic, Mariano Jose de Lara. He committed suicide at the age of 27, apparently for unrequited love. Many of his articles survived him, vividly describing the Madrid and the citizens of his time.

Influenced by the proximity of the Teatro Real, this district has a musical aura about it, seen in the shops for musical instruments and scores, and its many "coffee-concerts".

We will end this tour in Plaza Isabel II, or perhaps we can relax at the wooden tables of one of the restaurants. If the octopus looks a bit off putting, at least try the delicate wine which comes from here – the *Ribeiro*.

Iglesia de la Paloma – The Church of the Dove

Spiritual Madrid

Metro: Opera, Lines 2, 5.
Buses: 25, 33, 39.

On this tour, we will visit two convents which have collected important art treasures for generations. Art comprises a meeting of the physical and the spiritual, and is often the way through which the religious concept becomes human.

We start close to the Plaza de Oriente, at the **Plaza de la Encarnación**. The square is an intimate and peaceful place, with a statue of Lope de Vega at its center, preserving the atmosphere of the past. **Convento de la Encarnación** (the Convent) was founded in 1616 by Queen Margarita of Austria, the wife of Philip III. The interior design was renovated by Ventura Rodriguez in, 1767 and has been unchanged ever since. Its style is restrained, a characteristic of many buildings of that time, as is the combination of red brick and stone. The convent has an important **museum** containing paintings and statuary. Our visit to the museum starts at a small door in the west wing of the main façade. A tiny entrance, decorated with a few portraits, is the waiting room. Visits are with convent guides only. Open Tues., Wed. and Sat. 10:30am-1pm and 4-6pm, Fri. 10am-1:30pm, Sun. 11am-2pm; closed on Mon. and Fri. Entrance fee. Tel. 247-0510.

The first rooms contain an interesting exhibition which includes paintings by Palomino, Carducco, Jusepe de Ribera and others. In the Cloister there is an impressive portrayal of Jesus after the deposition from the cross, by Gregorio Fernández; in the first Chapel there are some interesting exhibits, such as a 16th century Florentine Madonna, a painting from 1657 by Lucas Jordan, a sculpture of Jesus by Michael Perronius and a lovely ivory crucifix.

After passing through the room containing the grave of the first Mother Superior of the convent, we reach a room containing holy

PLAZA DE LA ENCARNACION

vessels and various other holy items, such as a vial containing the blood of St. Pantaleón, which, according to tradition, turns liquid every July 27th. It is worthwhile to stop for a moment at the colored wooden sculptures by Salzillo and by Pedro de Mena, who is considered one of the finest woodcarvers in Spain. This type of sculpture is quite typical of Spain, and combines high drama with realism. The church itself is a fine example of 18th century architecture in Madrid. It was renovated by Ventura Rodríguez, one of Spain's finest architects, after a fire had caused considerable damage. The renovations were completed in 1767, with only the façade remaining from the original building.

We carry on along Calle de la Bola. This is a narrow street fairly typical of Madrid, and it leads us to Plaza Santo Domingo. This square, which was once one of the entrances to the city, is named for a monastery which was destroyed in the last century. An Inquisition courthouse also functioned here. Today there is only an underground car-park and noisy traffic. We cross the length of the square until we reach Calle Véneras and Plaza San Martín. Here we can see the Monte de Piedad Building (Mount of Mercy), in which the city's poor would pawn what little they still had from better times. Built in 1870, it today houses exhibitions which are worthy of a visit, as is the lovely interior courtyard.

Convento de las Descalzas Reales – note the lavish decor of walls and ceiling

From here we cross to nearby **Plaza de las Descalzas** (Square of the Barefooted). There is a quiet and aristocratic atmosphere here, and one of Madrid's most important sites: **Convento de las Descalzas Reales** (Convent of the Royal Barefooted Ones).

Open Tues.-Sat. 10:30am-12:30pm, 4-5:30pm; Sun. and public holidays 11am-1:30pm; closed Mon. Entrance fee. Tel. 521-2779. Guided tours.

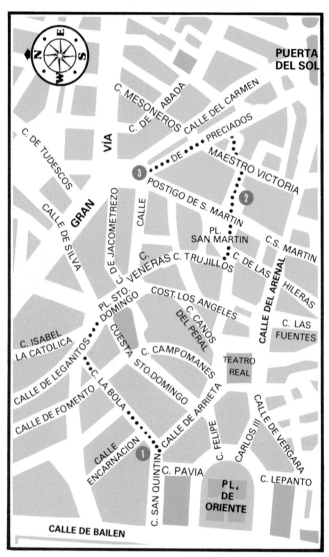

FROM PLAZA DE LA ENCARNACIÓN TO PLAZA DE CALLAO
1. Convento de la Encarnación
2. Convento de las Descalzas Reales
3. Plaza de Callao

This convent was founded by Princess Joanna of Austria at the court of the early kings of Castile. The princess herself was born here, "in the cold rooms of the Descalzas, facing the gardens", in the words of King Philip II. It is not certain when exactly it was built, but it is known that the work to turn it into a convent was carried out between 1556-1564. The façade – bricks and a mixture of sand, limestone and water – was constructed according to the building tradition of Madrid. The central gate, marking the church façade with a restrained line, is the work of the Escorial's first architect, Juan Battista de Toledo. Over the entrance is the coat of arms of the founding princess. Important women took refuge behind the walls of this convent including the Empress Isabel and her sister, St. Teresa of Avila. The royal nuns left many works of art in the palace, which have been preserved to this day.

We shall follow the fixed route. Notice that many of the works exhibited here depict children. Some are on subjects beloved to the painters of the Golden Age in Spain: the victory of Life over Death, symbolized by a child on a skeleton. In the waiting-room there are five 17th century, paintings by Bartolomé Román, depicting angels.

A feeling of tranquility and meditation at the Convento de las Descalzas Reales

The tour begins in a room holding many paintings and four altars in the corners. Among the outstanding paintings are a portrait of Carlos II by Claudio Coello, *Praise* by Miguel Barosso, and *The Holy Family* by Luis de Carvajal. From here we reach the magnificent main staircase, which is one of Madrid's finest baroque works.

There are several chapels in the high Cloister, all of which have many art treasures. In the first of them, we can see a depiction of Jesus after the Deposition by Gaspar Becerra from the 16th century. In the Capilla del Peñasco (Chapel of the Rock) there is a 17th century painting depicting the

The main staircase of the Convento de las Descalzas Reales – unusual baroque style elements

virgin with the baby Jesus, from the studio of Alonso Cano. On each side of the altar there are pictures of Jesus and of John the Baptist as children, by the same artist. In the Chapel of St. Michael you will see the painting of the child and the skeleton which we mentioned earlier.

From here we go to the Choir Room, with its collection of holy vessels. The nuns of the convent still use the Choir Room, and its most outstanding feature is the woodcarving of *La Dolorosa* by Pedro de Mena.

The next room is the Tapestry Room, with a breathtaking collection of tapestries woven after paintings by Rubens. The collection was donated to the convent in 1627. Its main theme is Jesus' Last Supper, and particularly impressive are the architectural background paintings. In the Dormition Chapel, the 16th century *Transito de la Virgen* is especially noteworthy.

A corner of worship at the Convento de las Descalzas Reales

The tour includes a visit to the Kings' Hall, where important visitors were received. On the left is one of the most important works of the entire collection – a 16th century painting by Pentuja de la Curce, of Empress Maria of Austria in nun's habit. Other rooms contain more exhibitions, such as Titian's *The Emperor's Coin* and several interesting Flemish works. The last place on the tour is the church – a lovely example of 16th century Spanish architecture.

Our route now undergoes a dramatic contrast, as we move to the heart of modern, commercial Madrid – to Calle Preciados, and from there to Plaza de Callao. Here we can finish our tour with a shopping spree, or just relax at one of the many cafés, and try to accustom ourselves once more to the sounds of the present, after the quiet and tranquil atmosphere of the convent.

The Twentieth Century

Metro: Callao, Lines 3, 5.
Buses: 1, 2, 44, 74, 75, M-2, M-3, M-4, M-5, M-10.

Plaza de Callao embodies all the signs of the 20th century – both the good and the bad: enormous department stores and hundreds of smaller shops representing the obsessive and ever-growing consumerism of big-city life; the movie-houses with their eye-catching pictures outside, mostly of violent scenes; the nightclubs, with large competitive billboards. The air of the city is polluted here by the Metro and the thousands of buses and cars. This is where the beggars gather, the blind tell fortunes, street musicians play, pavement artists draw, all watched over by the towering Palace of Journalism. We leave the square by the Gran Vía (Main Street) and turn right.

By the end of the 19th century, the necessity for a wide road, which would lead out of the labyrinth of narrow streets, had already been recognized. Work only began in 1910, and many streets were demolished to make way for the Gran Vía. In 1952, construction was completed on the last of the buildings which had been erected during the preceding 40 years in a variety of styles. The results are impressive indeed, if a little amusing at times – Spanish architectural imagination sometimes seems to run riot. To fully appreciate the wonders of the building here, look up: above a fairly "normal" edifice you will see statues of every kind of animal imaginable, mythological gods and goddesses, and even some creatures created expressly for the ornamentation of the buildings.

At the corner of Gran Vía and Calle Fuencarral is the Telephone Exchange, Madrid's first skyscraper (1929). An American architect who was invited to oversee its construction, brought with him new techniques in building. The design was that of a Spanish architect, who drew his inspiration from Madrid Baroque. Opposite the Exchange there is a small square, **Red de San Luis** (The Net of St. Luis), whose name apparently refers to the nets with which the bakers here used to cover their loaves. Calle Montero which leads off this square is named after a very beautiful lady

Plaza de Callao

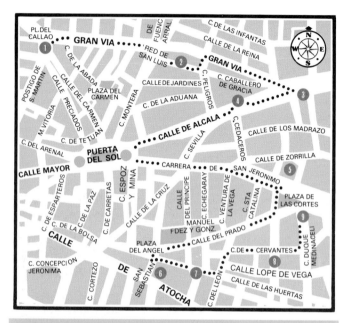

who was the wife of the King's chief artist, Montero, and whose appearances on her balcony caused riots (she was only watering the plants...). After she was the cause of a duel between a Marquis and a lieutenant of the Royal Guard, the Monteros were banished from their home, leaving behind them only the name of the street.

We shall make a little detour from the square and enter Calle Caballero de Gracia, parallel to the Gran Vía, to see a lovely church. This is the **Oratorio del Caballero de Gracia**, a small and harmonious building built by Juan de Villanueva in neo-classical style at the end of the 18th century. We return to the Gran Vía along Calle Virgen de los Peligros. From Callao to the beginning of the street, various architectural styles are on display. As we progress along the street we go back in time to where the street's construction began. While at the beginning of our tour we could see the dominant American influence, here buildings are more European style, neo-baroque, neo-classical, neo-Gothic. Look at nos. 1, 7, 10 and 12 – they are outstanding examples of these styles, all freely mixed together.

The Gran Vía by night

We now leave the Gran Vía and cross to Calle Alcalá, also wide, but unlike the rich new Gran Vía, which has an esteemed history. But Calle Alcalá has also changed its character. Once it was a meeting place for high society, the site of monasteries and palaces, and later, in the 19th century, respectable cafes and theaters. Today, the monumental banks set the tone, dominating everything else. Take a look, for instance, at the Banco Central at No. 45, (built by Palacios), Banco Mercantile de Industrial at No. 31, and the Banco de Bilbao at No. 16.

In contrast, there are also some buildings dedicated to the spirit. At Alcalá 42, Palacios built the **Círculo de Bellas Artes**

Puerta del Sol – the city's boundary till the 15th century

(Building of Fine Arts) in 1929, which we recommend visiting. Inside there are constant and varied cultural activities: theater, music, plastic arts, etc. Using a separate entrance, the building also houses a pretty café patronized by the participants in the various fine arts groups. Another building dedicated to the arts is the **Real Academia de Bellas Artes de San Fernando** (Royal Academy of San Fernando), at no. 13. Here the process was reversed: it was built by Churriguera in 1710 as the home of a wealthy banker. In 1752, King Fernando VI, influenced by ideas he brought back from his exile in France, decided to found an academy of fine arts, for the study of painting, sculpture and architecture. The building underwent a radical change in appearance in the spirit of the times, the baroque façade was made neo-classical, with Vianueva designing the alterations. Today the building holds a collection of paintings and sculpture, including works by El Greco, Zurbarán, Murillo, Goya and others. Open Tues.-Fri. 9am-7pm, Sat., Sun., Mon. and public holidays 9am-5pm. Entrance fee. Tel. 522-1491.

Going straight on, we reach **Puerta del Sol** (Sun Gate), the very heart of the city. The name of this gate apparently comes from the fact that this was one's point of arrival or departure when visiting the south. In the 15th century this was in fact the city boundary, but is now its center. A monastery courtyard, which has since disappeared, was called El

Plaza de Callao is surrounded by massive buildings

Mentidero ("the town's center for telling lies") – this was where people gossiped and formed conspiracies. With the passage of time, the gossip and the lies removed themselves to the cafes, from which the rebellious and the malcontents took to the streets. Many an historical event has taken place here: the uprising against the order to shorten all cloaks and make hats smaller (1766); the rebellion of May 2, 1808 against the forces of Napoleon; the stormy and enthusiastic reception of the Spanish-English-Portuguese army which had defeated Napoleon at the Battle of Arapiles in 1812, and others. In 1830, following a cholera epidemic, there was a popular uprising against the clergy, whom the people accused of poisoning the wells. Monasteries were burned, and men of the cloth were murdered. All this and more are part of Puerta del Sol's history – but gunfire and bloodshed are not the only features of this place: the Muses are heard here too. In these very same cafes, politics mixed with literature, people argued not only about government but also about poetry.

Puerta del Sol is also where progress began in Madrid. In 1830, gas-lighting was introduced here, in 1897 the first

tram-car, and in 1919, deep under this square, the first Metro line was opened. All roads begin here, quite literally – Puerta del Sol is Kilometer 0: all distances are measured from here, all street numbers begin from the end nearest here. And if Spain is the center of the world (as the Spaniards claim) and Madrid the center of Spain (geographically and politically), then Puerta del Sol must be the undisputed center of the Universe! And so it says, on an engraved stone on the sidewalk near the most important and interesting building in the vicinity: **Casa de Correos** (The Post Office). Its name discloses the original purpose for which it was built in 1760. Later it became the home of local government, and then it reached its darkest hour – as the Office of Civilian Security, which terrorized the citizens during Franco's reign. Here thousands of innocent people were tortured. Today it is once again the home of the local government.

Casa de Correos, today used by the local government

A high tower was added to the building about 100 years after its construction, containing a clock, and a ball which descends when the clock strikes twelve. On December 31, many of the inhabitants gather here to celebrate the New Year together. By tradition, as the clock strikes 12 they eat 12 grapes, one per chime. After the grapes ceremony – champagne and kisses.

On this festive note, we end this route, but not without first visiting somewhere pleasant and interesting with a good choice of restaurants and cafes. For this we have an entire street: Espoz y Mina, at the southeast corner of the square. Once you have relaxed here, you might wander to the end of the street, where you can buy tickets for the bull-fight.

Typically ornamented buildings at the Gran Vía

In the Footsteps of Lope de Vega

Metro: sol, Lines 1, 3, 5.
Buses: 3, 5, 15, 20, 50, 51, 52, 53, M-1, M-12.

This route is shown on the map in the previous chapter, "The Twentieth Century".

Our tour this time leaves from Puerta del Sol and passes along Carrera de San Jerónimo. This street has known better times – not that it is so disagreeable now, but it was once the route of royalty and aristocracy. Courtiers of the Church of Jerónimos in the Prado walked here, from their abode in the Eastern Palace – which is in the west. When the second palace, Buen Retiro, was built, the street was adorned with stages on which were performed shows, music and dancing. This entertainment went on here when the royal entourage passed by. Today, of course, the area is dominated by banks. But there is more besides banks: no. 6 houses a venerable institution – the restaurant and delicatessen *Lhardy*, founded in 1846 and known for its fine appearance and the delectable taste of its products. The upstairs section is more expensive, but those on a tight budget can order soup from the large samovar downstairs, or buy a few tasty morsels.

Another relic of the past is the **Palacio de Mirafloras**, at no. 15. This baroque building, built in 1732 by Pedro Ribera, was recently designated a national monument. It

The classic Spanish-American Bank

gives us the opportunity to examine one of the later works of Ribera, who designed many of Madrid's finest buildings. At the crossroads which form the Plaza Canalejas (named for a politician assassinated in Puerta del Sol) there are two interesting buildings. One is the **Banco Hispano Americano** (Spanish-American Bank), built solidly along classic lines, and the other, opposite, offering a sharp contrast, is the **Credit Lyonnais**, which has everything – brick, wood, stone, ceramics, embossments, recesses, a tower, a weathervane and many more

The colorful flags at the Spanish Parliament playfully contrast this neo-classical, solemn-looking building

features besides. Surprisingly, it doesn't look bad at all... The street ends with a royal fanfare – at **Palacio de las Cortes** (the Spanish Parliament). This neo-classical building has been the political center of Spain since 1850. Austere, and symmetrical, the entrance is adorned with two lions, cast from the iron of the cannons captured in the African War of 1860, in which Spain fought Morocco for the land she held – and still holds – in North Africa, Ceuta and Melilla. Spain won the war, but it brought her to her knees economically. In Plaza Cortes stands the statue of Spain's greatest author, Miguel de Cervantes Saavedra, forefather of the modern novel. This was the first statue in Madrid dedicated to a figure other than a king or saint.

We now turn into the Calle del Prado (not to be confused with the promenade bearing the same name, the Paseo del Prado). This street has been an important cultural center since the early 17th century. Even in the cafés you can hear classical music, and old books are on sale in more than one shop. One example of an important cultural institution is the *Ateneo*, at no. 21, where many a fierce battle was waged (and not only academically) on

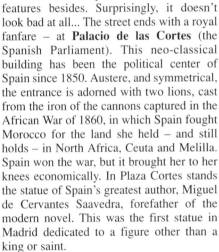

The Ateneo

behalf of freedom of speech and artistic expression.

Further along the street is the **Plaza de Santa Ana**, which like many others, owes its existence to the hated French king, Joseph Bonaparte. In the center, facing the **Teatro Español** (Spanish Theater), is a statue of the great dramatist **Calderón**, author of *La Vida Es Sueño* (*Life is a Dream*). There are some pleasant cafés in the square, such as the old *Cervecería Alemana*. The *Victoria Hotel* is here too, built in 1919, its shape reminiscent of the summer resorts frequented by the aristocracy at the beginning of the century. The Spanish Theater is the oldest in Europe; or to be more precise, it is the restored version of the oldest theater in Europe. The original theater was built in 1583 but burnt to the ground in 1802. The present building was opened in 1849, but in 1975 there was another fire. The façade was fortunately undamaged, and performances were resumed in 1980. Here the finest plays of the Golden Era and the Romantic period were staged. Today the performances are mostly classical dramas.

Lhardy, a restaurant and delicatessen which was founded in 1846

Before leaving the square, we shall take a quick look at

Manuel Fernández y Gonzalez Lane. There are several inns here whose walls, both inside and out, are lined with illustrated ceramic tiles and which are well worth a visit. Every Saturday evening there is a craft fair in the Plaza Santa Ana.

Close to Plaza Santa Ana is the **Plaza del Angel**, where there also used to be a *corral* (stage for performances). Today there is only a lovely café – *Café Central*, which has jazz combos playing in the evenings.

We now turn into Calle San Sebastian, where the **Iglesia de San Sebastián** stands. This was the church of Madrid's artists for

Plaza St. Ana and the Victoria Hotel

hundreds of years, and Spain's greatest dramatist, Lope de Vega, is buried here. He is one of cultural history's most fascinating figures. Whatever he did, he did to excess: he wrote thousands of plays and poems, loved many women, and was both a soldier and a clergyman. In his day, the center of life in Madrid was the theater, and Lope de Vega stood center-stage. Everyone talked and gossiped about him. His liaisons with actresses were common knowledge, and his love of them is expressed in his glorious poetry:

> *To face transparent disappointment*
> *To swallow poison as if it were a sweet potion*
> *To forget that which is good to us, to love the destructive*
> *To believe that Heaven's place is in Hell*
> *To give life and soul to despair*
> *This is love. He that has tasted it, knows it.*

This church is also connected with the memory of another poet – Jose Cadalso – and his love for the beautiful actress María Ignasia. He was a young poet, handsome and educated, and also a captain in the Spanish army. Their love blossomed, and the young poet decided to marry her, even though his friends looked down upon the alliance (acting was not considered a respectable profession in those days). The following spring, the actress died and the poet was heart-broken. On a gloomy night a few days after her death, he went into Iglesia de San Sebastián and dug up her grave. Suddenly the law burst into the church and arrested him. He was sent to Salamanca – not as a punishment, but in order to overcome his grief; but he never did, and all his most beautiful and most despairing poems are of his love. He died ten years later, in 1782, in the fortress on Gibraltar.

An exquisite wall mural by the Victoria Hotel

We shall continue on through Calle Huertas and its memories: here and in the neighboring streets lived Cervantes, Góngora, Queve-

The Church of San Sebastián – Lope de Vega, the famous dramatist, is buried here

do, Moratín and of course, Lope de Vega. No. 13 Calle Huertas is the **Ugena Palace**, today the Ministry of Commerce. The building's two façades face Calles Huertas and Príncipe. It was built in 1734 as part of Philip V's program to beautify the city – a program in which the aristocracy of the time participated. It is built in the Madrid version of the baroque style. Further along the street there is a small square called **Plaza de Matute** (Contraband), which used to be the site of a lively trade in smuggled goods. This dubious activity is no longer conducted here, but it is still worth a short visit.

Home of Lope de Vega – playwright, soldier and clergyman

At the corner of Calle Huertas and Calle León is the **Real Academia de la Historia** (Royal Academy of History), built in 1788. Turning into Calle León and then into Calle Cervantes, at no. 11 we find **Casa de Lope de Vega** (Lope de Vega House), home of the artist who has left his mark on the whole of Madrid. The house is open to visitors on Tues. and Thurs. 10am-2pm, closed from July 15 to Sept. 15. This is where Lope

De Vega wrote most of his works, and the house has been reconstructed and preserved as it was when he lived there. Lope De Vega lived out his last years here, years full of suffering after his last wife died from mental illness. His troubles did not end here, and some say that as a punishment for his youthful Don Juan ways, his beloved daughter was kidnapped by another Don Juan, named Tenorio.

We carry on along Calle Cervantes as far as the Duque de Medinace, turn left, and there we see the grand edifice of the *Hotel Palace* – an elegant hotel built in 1912, patronized by many of the most important visitors, such as the infamous Mata Hari. We can end our tour seated in comfort at the magnificent *Art Nouveau Bar.*

From Plaza de Neptuno to the "Low Districts"

Buses: 14, 27, 34, M-6.

This tour starts in the Plaza Cánovas del Castillo, better known to the locals as **Plaza de Neptuno**, after the fountain of the god of the sea which adorns its center. We turn into Calle Cervantes and then left to Plaza de Jesús, where we see the **Iglesia de Jesús de Medinacelli**. This church, which is fairly new, is not particularly interesting architecturally, but contains an image of Jesus much loved by the city's residents, who flock there especially on Fridays in March. During this month, long lines of believers come to ask for three wishes – of which, it is said, one will always be fulfilled. Around the square there is a lively trade in holy artifacts and statuettes.

We carry on along Calle Jesús to Calle Moratín, named for the. 18th century dramatist who once lived here. We then reach Calle Atocha, and cross it. At the corner on the right is one of Madrid's oldest cinemas, *Cine Doré*, which was built in 1923. We turn right at Calle Santa Isabel and reach **Plaza de Antón Martín.** This tiny square has been frequently altered, and today bears no resemblance to any of its previous incarnations. A historical uprising took place here in 1766 during the reign of Carlos III. The king's powerful aide, the Marquis of

Cine Doré – Madrid's oldest cinema

Esquilache, ordered the citizens of Madrid to shorten their cloaks and make their hats smaller. This strange decree was issued to

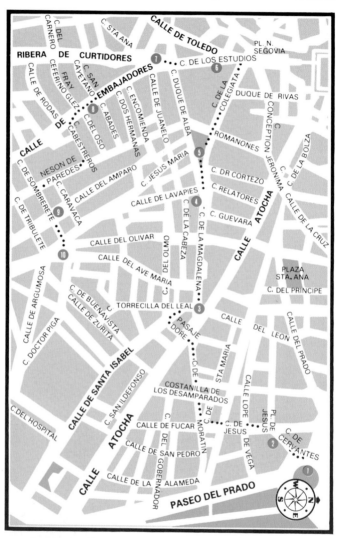

FROM PLAZA DE NEPTUNO TO THE "LOW DISTRICTS"

1. Plaza de Neptuno
2. Iglesia de Jesús de Medinacelli
3. Plaza de Antón Martín
4. Palacio de Perales
5. Plaza de Tirso de Molina
6. Catedral de San Isidro
7. Plaza de Cascorro
8. Iglesia de San Cayetano
9. La Corrala building
10. Plaza de Lavapiés

stop the citizens from hiding their faces under their wide-brimmed hats and from concealing their weapons under their cloaks. On March 23, in this square, near the army barracks which used to be here, two men wrapped in long cloaks and wearing round hats stationed themselves. The guards warned them that they could not stand there, but they made no response. Suddenly a loud whistle was heard, and thirty men miraculously appeared out of nowhere and grabbed the soldiers' weapons. Within a short time the whole city was involved in the uprising. The king finally rescinded the order. Following this event, Carlos III threatened to remove the capital from Madrid, but retracted the decision.

In the Iglesia de Jesús de Medinacelli – an apsis with Moslem influences

There is something more tangible than anecdotes from the past on this square, namely, **Cine Monumental**, the large auditorium built in 1923, with very unusual acoustics. Here, for the first time in the city's history, reinforced concrete was used in construction.

Calle Magdalena, which branches out from Plaza de Antón Martín, many years ago was the road running between olive groves to the Shrine of the Virgin of Atocha (which we will visit on our next tour). The road itself was also lined with small shrines, one of which is dedicated to Mary Magdalene, whose road to sanctification was a long one. During the reign of Philip II, several monasteries and palaces were built. With the exception of **Palacio de Perales** (marquis of Perales Palace) none of these remain in this busy commercial street today. This baroque edifice was built in 1732 and designed by Ribera. The esteemed Marquis himself was thrown from its large balcony in 1808, by an angry crowd led by the orange-seller Pepa. At that time, the Marquis was Governor of

Madrid, and the people accused him of collaborating with the French conqueror and ordering the distribution of sand-filled ammunition to the rebels.

Further along we come to **Plaza de Tirso de Molina**, named for the dramatist who created the character Don Juan. This popular square fills with people in the late morning hours, especially on Sundays. As well as the usual commercial commodities, here you can also trade in political opinions, and buy books, pamphlets, badges and posters, most sharing a common hatred of Americans.

The statue of the famous dramatist, Tirso de Molina, in the square honoring his name

We carry on along Calle Colegiata, whose left side is the side wall of the **Catedral de San Isidro**. We turn into Calle Estudios to enter the impressive cathedral. Construction of the cathedral and seminary was begun in 1622 by the Jesuit Order. During the reign of Carlos III the Jesuits were banished from Spain, and the king ordered the architect Rodriguez to adapt the interior of the cathedral to new requirements. The remains of St. Isidro and his wife were transferred here, and the cathedral was declared the Royal Church.

Back on Calle Estudios, we soon reach **Plaza de Cascorro**. This is where the *Rastro*, the flea market of Madrid, begins. It is also the entrance to the city's "low life". A statue of Eloy Gonzalo stands in the middle of the square. He is standing with a jerrycan of oil under his arm in memory of his brave deed: during the Cuban war he set fire to the enemy's camp. The Spanish commemorate not only victories, but also defeats – a hero is a hero, and the outcome is of less significance. In that impossible war, the Spanish fought the Americans so bravely, that it is said that the victors were filled with respect and admiration for the heroism of the vanquished.

We walk down Calle Embajadores (Ambassadors Street), named for an event which happened here in the Middle Ages, when King Juan II met a group of ambassadors in Madrid. An epidemic of the plague had broken out, one of many which afflicted Europe, and in order to distance themselves from danger, the ambassadors met here in this street, which at the time was some way from the city.

The impressive Catedral de San Isidro, built in the style of the Jesuit order

We descend with the slope of the street: "the low districts" refers not only to its topography, but also to the socio-economic level of its residents. At no. 15 is the **Iglesia de San Cayetano** (Church of San Cayetano), creation of the baroque architects of Madrid, Churriguera and his disciple Pedro de Ribera. Only the façade and entrance hall remain of the original church, built in 1722 – a fire destroyed the interior in 1936. It has now been rebuilt, but what was lost could not be reconstructed. We continue to the corner of Calles Embajadores and Cabestreros, where we can see a house which appears to be of one story only, but stepping back a little, you will see that in fact it has three. This is one of the "crafty houses", built in this way to get around the seventeenth century law which obliged owners of multi-storied buildings to "donate" one story to royal courtiers. We now turn onto Calle Cabestreros (Harness-Makers Street). Here a tradition developed of feeding domestic animals with barley that had been blessed, as a remedy against disease. Cows and horses were also given water from the fountain. The fountain stands at the end of the street, and is accredited with properties which will increase virility – not only of animals. Try it and see!

The busy and lively Calle Mesón de Paredes

We have now reached Calle Mesón de Paredes – forever bustling, it has something mischievous and gay about it, almost rustic. It has many eating places and inns, the oldest of which is at no. 14 – *Antonio Sanchez*. We go down here as far as Calle Sombrerete – meaning "little hat", in memory of the cap of shame placed on the head of the priest, when he claimed that his friend the baker was none other than the King of Portugal who had disappeared in battle. The priest was hanged, and the hat still on his lifeless head was remembered by the people, who later gave its name to the street. At the corner between the two streets there is a charming square, with **La Corrala** building at one side. This is a typical example of the kind of building popular in the nineteenth century, and it is apparently a stage set for the Zarzuela. And indeed, you can see Spanish operettas here. It stands next to the ruins of what was once a church and school, ruins which have been left as they are.

Continuing along Calle Sombrerete we soon reach **Plaza de Lavapíes**, which we will discuss in the next tour. In the meantime, we can buy something sweet in Calle Caravaca, which runs parallel to it. At no. 10 there is a delicatessen called *El Madroño*, named after a fruit which was so popular here that it became the symbol of the city, together with the bear, (which also enjoyed the fruit). Today there are no bears, and almost no *madroño* trees. Of the fruit of the few remaining trees, this little delicatessen makes pies and wine – taste them, and get to know the real flavor of Madrid.

A quiet corner in the Lavapiés neighborhood – the heart of Madrid

From here it is not far to the **Rastro**. For those of you who are ready to really rub shoulders with the *Madrileños* in a very special experience, we suggest a walk and shopping spree in this famous market. Here are a few pointers – what, where and when. Remember: keep a tight hold on your purse or wallet, as well as your temper. And always haggle over prices!

Handling a bargain is easy in the Rastro, handling the purchase seems not quite as easy

The market is open on Sundays, and the best hours of the day, when it is still possible to breathe – are early morning (meaning 11am – before that there is nothing) and after 2pm. At 3pm the stallholders pack up.

In the main street, Ribera de Curtidores, you can buy objets d'art; jewelry, textiles and dolls, and various other bargains such as leather goods.

In Plaza Vara del Rey you will find antiques and other old artifacts, stones and shells.

In Calle Rodrigo Guevara – used (and very used) clothing is sold, and you can sometimes find some very interesting garments, such as matador costumes or a glittering evening dress from years ago. In Calle Mira del Rio Alta – second-hand goods of every kind imaginable can be found.

The Rastro is a charming spot which provides a perfect opportunity for last-minute shopping

Plaza de Campillo del Mundo Nuevo has books, plants and gardening accessories, medicinal herbs and spices.

Arts and Sciences – From Plaza de Lavapiés to the Botanical Gardens

Metro: Lavapiés, Line 3.

Plaza de Lavapiés, the very heart of bustling Madrid, is the starting point for this route. The whole district, also called Lavapiés (Washing of the Feet), was apparently once the Jewish Quarter, until the Jews were expelled from Spain in 1492. After that, the residents of the neighborhood were Jews who had already converted to Christianity, and people who moved to Madrid from other areas of Spain.

The nickname *Manolo*, which is given to the people who live here, stems from the tradition among the converted of naming their first-born sons Emmanuel. The literature of the time characterizes the *Manolos* as quick-tempered, aggressive and proud, with a tendency to exaggerate – and first class talkers. In time, *Manolos* became *Chulos* – which philologists say comes from the Arabic word *chaul*, meaning "lad". Yet another nickname used for these people is *majo* (or *maja* for a girl), meaning "smart" or "dashing", which is a distortion of *mayo*. Since neighborhood beauties were traditionally chosen in May, the people used to dress up in their best clothes, and as time went by, the term *majo* or *maja* came to mean any well-dressed, smart-looking person. The name of the square itself is the subject of many a learned discussion, but clearly it is connected with water, perhaps a fountain, or the water which doubtlessly collected here after heavy rains when water flowed down the steep Calles Olivar, Lavapiés and Ave María. In recent times the square has become a favorite spot for young Bohemians. It is full of life in the evenings, and its various pubs and bars have a very cultured atmosphere. During the day, this is simply a pleasant and ordinary neighborhood.

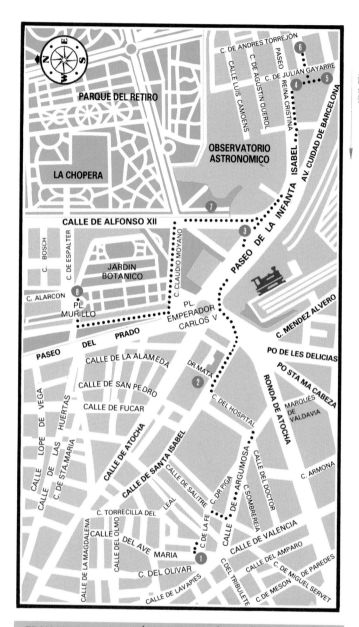

FROM PLAZA DE LAVAPIÉS TO THE JARDÍN BOTÁNICO

1. Plaza de Lavapiés
2. Hospital General de San Carlos
3. Museo Nacional de Etnología
4. Panteón de Hombres Ilustres
5. Basílica de Atocha
6. Real Fábrica de Tápices
7. Observatorio Astronómico
8. Jardín Botánico

We turn into Calle de la Fe (faith street). This was once the main street of the *Judería* (Jewish Quarter), and at one end, where the San Lorenzo Church stands, there used to be a synagogue. The street's name was given after the expulsion of the Jews – and it is unclear whether the reference is to the faith of those who remained or of those who were expelled. The church, which is on the corner of Calle Salitre, is very simple, and known around here as "The Church of the Fleas", but it is nevertheless one of the most popular churches in Madrid. The original building was erected in 1660, but was completely destroyed by fire. The present building was built on the ruins in 1851.

Plaza de Lavapiés

Calle Salitre is named for the warehouses of saltpeter which once stood here (saltpeter was used in making gunpowder). From here we turn left into Calle Argumosa. This wide and shady street is that of the district's "aristocracy". Argumosa was a fine doctor at the time of Queen Isabel II, and the streets on both sides of Argumosa are also named after doctors. We now turn left into Calle Hospital, and indeed the huge building here was originally the **Hospital General de San Carlos**. It was built in the 18th century as part of the plan of Carlos III for enlarging the city. He envisaged concentrating under one roof all the small medical institutions strewn over the city. He appointed Sabatini, one of the palace architects, to plan the hospital, and part of it was indeed built according to Sabatini's design. In 1831 the Faculty of Medicine, Pharmacy and Surgery was founded next to the hospital, again planned by Sabatini. In 1986 the hospital became an art center, on the initiative and in the name of Queen Sophia – **Centro de Arte Reina Sofia**. It exhibits modern art – not only paintings and sculpture, but also music, video, design and more. The most famous exhibit here is probably Picasso's *Guernica*. Open Mon.-Wed. 10am-9pm. Closed Tues. Entrance fee. Tel. 467-5062.

At the Atocha Railway Station

The *Guernica* is one of the most important works to have been painted in the 20th century. In 1937, at the height of the Civil War, the Republican Government commissioned a painting from Picasso for the international exhibition in Paris. Several months went by, and the artist had not found a suitable subject for his painting, until, at the end of April, the world heard of the bombardment of the Basque town Guernica by Nazi bombers in the service of the Spanish Fascists. Guernica – far from any military target – became the symbol of Basque freedom. On May 1st, Picasso began the first sketches for his work, and had finished them by the end of June.

The painting is not a realistic portrayal of the event, but a combination of fragmentary cubist images in black, white and gray. A screaming mother rushes out with a dead child in her arms, disembodied heads and arms express terror and anguish, and the head of a bull looms above, perhaps a symbol of irrational force in man. The hand holding up a lamp represents resistance to the powers of evil and destruction. This painting has become more than a memorial to the destruction of Guernica; it is also a powerful protest against the cruelty and terror of man's darker side. Following Franco's victory, and in the face of the threat of the Nazi conquest of Paris, Picasso gave the painting to the Museum of Modern Art in New York, stipulating that it should remain there until democracy returned to Spain.

We now leave the peaceful atmosphere of the museum and plunge into the never-ending tumult of the **Glorieta del Emperador Carlos V** (the Square of King Carlos V). The most important thing in this square is the **Atocha Railway Station**, and, in fact, everybody refers to the square by this name. This handsome building is constructed of iron and glass in the finest Art Nouveau or Modernismo style. The first train departed from here in 1851, and its passenger of honor was Queen Isabel II. The train traveled to the royal resort town of Aranjuez, and on the way, young girls distributed strawberries, the principal produce of the town. Since then the line has been known as the "strawberry train". The custom has been revived in recent years, and in the spring and summer the strawberry train travels between Madrid and Aranjuez carrying the young girls and their

The Atocha Railway Station was constructed in Modernismo style

The Ministry of Agriculture

strawberries. The square itself could have been quite attractive: it is spacious, has a lovely fountain, and plenty of popular eating places, but the traffic is terribly noisy, because of the many buses connecting the north of the city with the south which stop here, and because of the taxis which constantly come and go from the station.

Carefully crossing the vehicles area, we come to an interesting building: the **Ministry of Agriculture**, at No. 1 Calle Infanta Isabel. It was erected in 1893, and is noteworthy for its use of many and varied materials: the walls are of stone, the pillars of marble, over the building there are winged horses cast in bronze, and the walls are decorated with colored ceramic tiles. We walk a little further along this street, and at the corner of Calle Alfonso XII, will see the *Statuettes on exhibit at* **Museo Nacional de Etnología** (Ethnological *the Ethnological* cal Museum). Open Tues.-Sat. *Museum* 10am-7:30pm, Sun. 10am-2pm. Closed Mon. and public holidays. Entrance fee. Tel 530-6418.

This museum is the fruit of the labors of one man: the famous doctor and anthropologist, Pedro Gonzáles Velasco, who invested all his energies and wealth in its establishment. He was known to be a strange man, and the imaginative and babbling citizens of Madrid spun countless legends around him. The most popular one concerned his daughter, whom he loved to distraction. Sadly, the girl died young, giving rise to the story (which was denied, in vain), that the doctor mummified her body and continued to act as though she were still alive: sat her with him for meals, and went with her for rides in their carriage, with the body dressed in the height of fashion. But, as is often the case, many legends develop about learned people, as if they had something of the devil in them, something profane and threatening.

The lovely building was officially opened in 1875 after the death of its founder, and here

The Ethnological Museum, founded by Velasco in 1875

you can find fascinating collections of tools, models of houses, statues of the gods of American, African, Asian and Oceanian peoples, and a collection of mummies from the Canary Islands and other places.

We now continue along the right-hand side of the Paseo de la Reina Cristina (Queen

At the Pantheon

Cristina Promenade), as far as the corner of Calle Gayarre. At this corner is the **Panteón de Hombres Ilustres**. This is the eternal resting place of the great figures of Spain. The history of the place is both comic and macabre, and reveals the peculiar nature of Spanish politics and society. In 1837 it was decided at the *Cortes* to erect a national pantheon at the church of San Francisco el Grande (see "The Western Districts"), and the Academy of History was appointed to select the pantheon's "inhabitants". For 32 years nothing was done. In 1869 the initiative was renewed, this time with an appointed committee. But the committee came up against an insurmountable obstacle: the bodies of the illustrious dead could not be found. It was well known, for instance, that Cervantes was buried at the Trinitarias Monastery, but nobody knew exactly where; Lope de Vega was mislaid somewhere in the Church of San Sebastián, and the same for Velazquez at San Juán. Eventually, the remains of 14 important figures were found, but some could not be located. With great pomp and ceremony, with carriages and trumpet salvos, the remains were brought to the Holy Church – and there forgotten, until they were finally returned to their original burying-places. The years rolled by, and in the 19th century the pantheon was built, and once again the VIPs had to be chosen. But political arguments and intrigues made the work impossible. Laid to rest there today – and doubtless not eternally – are some military figures and politicians, beneath the showy statues in the dismal and empty baroque building. All of which goes to show that in Spain even the dead have no rest, and certainly no resting-place!

Near the pantheon stands the **Basílica de Atocha**. This building too has its legend. The Virgin of Atocha was the object of worship and admiration during the times of Moslem rule in Madrid. According to the legend, in the eighth century a Madrid knight found among the Spanish papyrus reeds (*atochas*) an image of the Virgin, and built a shrine in her honor. The Moslems discovered the shrine, and decided to attack the site. When the knight heard of the plan, he gathered a few brave men about him and prepared for battle, but he feared defeat. In particular, he feared for his wife and two daughters, who were liable to fall into the hands of the infidels and be dishonored. In an act of loving despair, he killed them before leaving for battle. However, luck was on the side of the Christians, who were victorious. The heart-broken knight entered the shrine, and there a surprise awaited him: the three women, alive and well, were kneeling beside the statue of the Virgin, with only a red mark around their necks and a puddle of blood at their feet as evidence of what had happened. The Virgin of Atocha became the beloved of the citizens of Madrid and the area, and over the years many churches and

The Pantheon – despite grandeous plans to bury Spain's finest, today only a few politians and some military figures are buried here

At the Royal Tapestry Factory – tapestries are woven or restored, based on famous artists' sketches

Browsing for second and third hand books at one of the many stalls on Calle Cuesta de Moyano

monasteries have been built in the vicinity. Only one rather uninspired building remains, built in the 1940's, after all the others had been burnt to the ground during the Civil War of 1936.

In contrast to the spiritual memories of the past there is something in nearby Calle Fuenterrabía which unites the past and the present: the **Real Fábrica de Tápices** (Royal Tapestry Factory). It was opened in 1721, and Spain's greatest artists, including Goya, drew the sketches on which the tapestries were based. A factory guide (who speaks only Spanish) will accompany visitors to the workshops, where the practised and nimble-fingered artists work at the ancient looms, just as their predecessors worked 400 years ago. Tapestries are woven according to the paintings of the greatest artists, and repairs are also done on old and worn tapestries. This is a highly recommended visit. Open Mon.-Fri. 9am-12:30pm. Closed Sat., Sun. and August. Entrance fee. Tel. 551-3400.

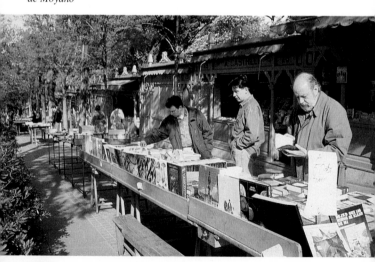

We now return to Calle Alfonso XII. On the right, at the corner of the Retiro Park, there is a path which leads us to the top of a small hill, to the **Observatorio Astronómico** (Observatory). This is one of the loveliest Spanish neo-classical buildings, and it was built by Vianueva in 1790 at the request of Carlos III. Of classic proportions and

symmetry, it is both simple and elegant, and contains a modest exhibition of ancient astronomy instruments. The hill is a lovely observation point over the city.

Paseo del Prado, a favorite amongst the Madrileños

Further along Calle Alfonso XII is the steep Calle Cuesta de Moyano, which is lined with second and third-hand bookstalls. During Franco's time, if you looked carefully under the stacks, you could find at these stalls, which have lately been renovated, the books banned by the authorities. At the top of the street there is a statue of Moyano himself, responsible for the compulsory education law, surprisingly erected in the appropriate place. Why surprisingly? Because in Madrid, statues, like the dead, are given no rest, but are moved from place

An imposing statue at the Botanical Gardens, in the Paseo del Prado

to place with an unexplained lack of logic. From here we walk onto the Paseo de Prado (Prado Promenade).

The lovely **Paseo del Prado** was already a favorite spot for *Madrileños* in the 16th century. Even though at the time there was a foul-smelling channel running down its center, to the sides there were groves of trees and beautiful gardens. We owe the promenade as we see it today to the Mayor King, Carlos III, who contributed so much to the beauty of the city. Helping him achieve his ambitions were the greatest architects of the time, Villanueva, Sabatini and Rodriguez. In accordance with the king's plan, the channel was drained and closed, the street was widened, and elaborate fountains were installed. He ordered the Observatory built, the Botanical Gardens and the Museum of Natural Sciences (today the Prado). The Promenade became the meeting place for anyone who was anyone. The most noticeable of these – and they really were noticeable, with their voluminous and fancy dresses – were the ladies of the royal court, always accompanied by their young admirers. Magnificent and fashionable clothes were their chief concern. The central figure among them was the mischievous and lovely Duchess of Alba. On one occasion, she learned that the Queen was going to appear at the Prado wearing a very special gown which she had received directly from Paris. Cayetana (the Duchess) sent her spies to the palace, and ordered four exact replicas from fast-working seamstresses. On the appointed day, the Queen appeared at the Prado, all smiles and pround as a peacock. Suddenly a carriage stopped, and the Queen fainted: four of the Duchess' maid-servants descended from the carriage, all wearing exactly the same dress as the Queen! Cayetana knew that her joke would cost her dearly, but she could always find refuge with her friend, the artist Goya.

We carry on along the promenade as far as

the Plaza Murillo, where we enter the **Jardín Botánico** (Botanical Gardens). Open summer – 10am-8pm; winter – 10am-6pm. Entrance fee. Tel. 585-4700. The gardens' collection includes about 30,000 varieties of trees, shrubs and plants. The sheer loveliness of the gardens, with their shade and their peaceful atmosphere, attracts many visitors. Until a few years ago, anyone wanting them could receive medicinal herbs here free of charge. The custom has been discontinued, but you can still buy some dried herbs at the shop at the entrance, as well as pictures and books on botany. Let's take a rest here amid the greenery before our next tour.

Beautiful red tulips at the Botanical Garden

The Prado Museum and the Retiro Gardens

Metro: Banco, Line 2.
Buses: 10, 14, 27, M-6.

The Prado Museum is considered to be one of the world's finest. It consists of two separate buildings: The Casón del Buen Retiro, which contains many 19th and early 20th century paintings, and the main building, planned by the architect Juan de Villanueva, with its breath-taking collection of paintings, sculpture and jewelry.

The museum is open Tues.-Sat. 9am-7pm; Sun. and public holidays 9am-2pm. Closed on Mon. The ticket includes entry to the Casón de Buen Retiro. On Sat. entrance is free. Free admission for persons under 21 years of age (members of the EEC) and for students. Tel. 420-2836.

Construction of the main building began in 1785, and was planned as a huge center for the study of the natural sciences. During the reign of Fernando VII, (inspired by his second wife, who loved art), the museum changed its designation and became the home of the country's finest art treasures. Despite the changes made to its structure, its original form has been scrupulously retained: the balanced neo-classical façade combines brick and granite in complete harmony. Facing it stands a statue of

The statue of Velázquez in front of the Prado Museum

Velázquez, by Marinas. The northern façade guards a statue of Goya by Mariano Benlliurie, and between the southern façade and the entrance to the Botanical Gardens there is a statue of Murillo.

It was Joseph Bonaparte who originated the idea of a museum of painting which would be open to the public. The museum was opened in 1819, after the war – "except on rainy days when people might bring in mud". At the

At the Prado Museum

time of its opening, the museum's collection consisted of 311 paintings, donated by the royal family and included works by Velázquez and Murillo. The "immodest" paintings which had been held in closed galleries of the Academy until then, were added to the collection. These included works by Titian and Rubens. In 1868, the year in which the museum was nationalized, the collections grew, thanks to the contributions of secularized monasteries. Today the museum owns about 6000 paintings – some on exhibition, some in storage, and some on tour in regional museums in Spain.

The museum is constantly being reorganized and reconstructed. We have therefore decided not to specify the names and locations of the renowned works of art exhibited here. The wealth of this superb museum makes it advisable to check for updated details on entrance and plan the visit according to your own preference and taste.

EL CASÓN DE BUEN RETIRO

4 Calle Felipe, which houses mostly 19th-century Spanish art, was once the ballroom of the royal palace. It was built in 1637, and to this day retains the ceiling painted by Lucas Jordan in the

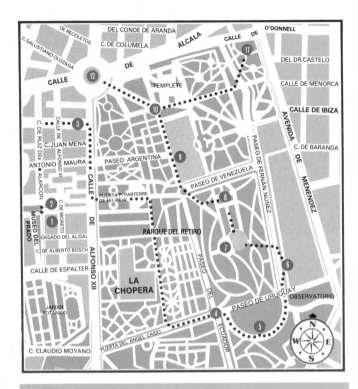

central hall. Open Tues.-Sat. 9am-7pm; Sun. and public holidays 9am-2pm; Closed on Mon. Tel. 420-2628.

Behind the Prado there is a hill, on which stands the impressive neo-Gothic **Iglesia de los Jerónimos** (Church of Los Jerónimos). The present building owes its appearance to renovations, improvements and additions which were added in the last century and after the Civil War. Right next to it you can see what remains of the 17th century cloister. The building you see from the porch, on the right, is the **Real Academia**

de la Lengua Española (Royal Academy of the Spanish Language), which was built in 1891 in neo-Classical style. The Academy itself has been in existence since 1714. Its function is to maintain the purity of the language, and to sift out mutations. The institution's motto is: "To clean, to determine, to add luster". Some years ago, a shoe polish company adopted the same motto, until the irate Academy brought suit against them. The 36 members of the Academy, who hold their discussions, seated in velvet armchairs, in this building, have the right to determine what you may and may not say (linguistically, that is), and nothing that they publish is subject to any kind of censorship – which in the past was a matter of great importance. Members of the Academy are elected for life, and only on the death of one member is another elected. This seems the appropriate moment to say a word about the Spanish language: in actual fact, many forms of Spanish are spoken in Spain. The standard form is Castilian, the language of Castile, but Catalan, Basque and Galician are also Spanish languages.

Iglesia de los Jerónimos

In the Casón del Buen Retiro

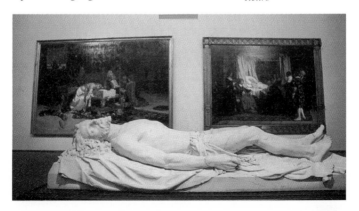

We now exit to Calle Ruiz de Alarcón and turn right along Calle Montalbán and again turn right. The "Jerónimos" district where we now find ourselves is an exclusive neighborhood, which is clearly evident by the architecture, most of which dates from the last century. At 12 Calle Montalbán is the **Museo Nacional de Artes Decorativos** (National Museum of Decorative Art), with its exhibits on ceramics, leather, jewelry, embroidery and furniture from various places and periods in Spain. Open Tues.-Fri. 10am-8pm, Sat. and Sun. 10am-2pm; closed on Mon. and public holidays. Entrance fee. Tel. 532-6499.

Parque del Retiro

Back again on Calle Montalbán we turn right into Calle Alfonso XII, and continue as far as the **Iglesia del Retiro** (Retiro Church) to the second gate, called the Puerta de Felipe IV. The Retiro Gardens and the Casón del Buen Retiro (see "The Prado"), together with the Military Museum (see below), are all that remain of a large complex intended for the rest and recreation of the royal family. The complex was built in 1633, during the reign of Philip IV, on land that he received as a gift from the Duke of Oliveras, who wished to increase his influence over the weak-willed and pleasure-loving king and promised him "a place for pleasure and laziness". Ironically enough, the name given to the place – Buen Retiro – means "retreat", borrowed from the name of the estate kept by the devoutly Christian King Philip II for fasting and prayer. In Philip IV's time, magnificent celebrations were held in the park, including

The interior of the Prado Museum

A tranquil spot in the Retiro

plays – on water, in the air and on dry land – their main purpose being to surprise the audience with dazzling effects.

The Retiro opened its doors to the public in 1868. Today it is a park for casual meetings, relaxation, sport, walking the dog, playing with the children and so on. Fairs are held here, movies are shown in the summer, and every Sunday it fills with street artists playing, dancing, performing, giving puppet shows and painting. We enter the park via Philip IV Gate, built during his reign. Facing us is the obsessive symmetry so typical of the rococo style: no item in this part of the park – called the **Parterre** (flower-bed) – grows wild. Living matter is moulded here by the hands of the creator, just like the stone and marble incorporated in it. We shall turn right along one of the paths and enter the forest called **La Chopera** (the Poplar Forest), which contrasts so sharply with the tended gardens – trees are hard to subjugate! In the center of the forest there are playgrounds, running tracks and a busy sports center. This is where the movies are shown in summer.

Having crossed La Chopera we reach an avenue where we turn left. At this corner there is the only statue in the world dedicat-

Feeding ducks at the Retiro Park – a pleasant pastime for adults and children alike

ed to Satan – **El Angel Caído** (The Fallen Angel). Immediately past it, on the right-hand side of the same avenue, is the lovely rose garden, **La Rosaleda** – a scented and multi-colored celebration. Further on, we cross the avenue and turn left, into the entrance of the quiet **Jardines de Cecilio Rodríguez** (Cecilio Rodríguez Gardens). Crossing the road again (this is where the fairs are held), we carry straight on. Beside the small lake is the **El Palacio de Cristal** (Crystal Palace), with a charming little spot next to it which is popular with young couples. Inside El Palacio de Cristal which was built in 1887 as a greenhouse, and in the nearby **Palacio de Velázquez** (Velázquez Palace) built in the same year, exhibitions are held. Beautiful ceramic tiles adorn this elegant building. We now go out to the **lake** – a perfect square, with a few boats and ducks, and fish fighting for their lives. On the other side of the lake a white complex attracts the eye, reminiscent of a frosted wedding cake. This is the monument dedicated to Alfonso XII.

At the far end of the lake there is a lovely fountain, the **Fuente de la Alcachofa** (Artichoke Fountain). It was designed by Ventura Rodríguez as part of the series of fountains along the Prado Promenade. Until about a

100 years ago it stood at Atocha, but was later transferred to its present site.

Another charming corner of the park, at the north-east end, is the artificially-built hill with its **ruins** of a 12th-century monastery brought from Avila, **waterfalls**, and a fantasy called **La Casita del Pescador** (The Fisherman's Cottage).

We leave the park via the main gate, which leads us to **Plaza de la Independencia**. One can, of course, stay longer in the Retiro – there's no hurry. Try to see the park in the fall – the colors are unbelievable!

One of Rodríguez's fountains in the Paseo del Prado

Along the Paseo de Recoletos

Metro: Retiro, Line 2.
Buses: 15, 28, M-2, M-8.

Plaza de la Independencia (Independence Square) is located at the north-western side of the Retiro Gardens. In the center of the square stands the **Puerta de Alcalá** (Alcalá Gate). This was the eastern border of Madrid until the middle of the 19th century. King Carlos III had ordered the architect Sabatini to build a gate which would ennoble the entrance to the city – especially as the king lived at the time in the nearby Retiro Palace. Since completion of the construction of the palace, there have been two assassination attempts here: the first on the life of King Fernando VII, (after which the assailant's head was proudly displayed), and the second in 1921 on the life of the prominent politician Eduardo Detto, by anarchists. The square is unblemished and extremely impressive.

Puerta de Alcalá – the eastern border of Madrid until the 19th century

We shall walk along the right side of the broad Calle Alcalá until we reach *Café Lion*, which during the twenties was the political and ideological center for young Madrid intellectuals. García Lorca and his poet friends, as well as people of the Left wing, used to meet on the ground floor, while in the basement the Spanish Phalanges were founded, under the leadership of Primo de Rivera. Poets still gather in the basement for

The fountain at Plaza de la Cibeles

a "*Taratolia*", but this wonderful institution – an informal meeting in a café for the discussion of ideas, poetry readings, the planning of revolutions and the forming of conspiracies – has disappeared from the scene, although many Spaniards are trying hard to resurrect it. A few steps further on we come to **Plaza de la Cibeles**, known locally simply as "La Cibeles", and considered to be the symbol of the city for other nations. Each part of the statue which crowns the fountain was sculpted by a different artist, with the whole overseen by none other than Ventura Rodriguez. The square itself is surrounded by monumental and impressive buildings. On the other side of Calle Alcalá there is a building which might surprise you: the **Palacio de Comunicaciones** (Communications Palace). Built in 1919 by a young architect named Antonio Palacios, it attempted to combine the latest construction techniques with an appearance which included almost every Spanish effect from every period. The result astounded the citizens, and they reacted to the strange edifice with typical humor, calling it "The Holy Virgin of Communications".

On the far side of the Paseo del Prado (Prado Promenade) is the **Banco de España** (Bank

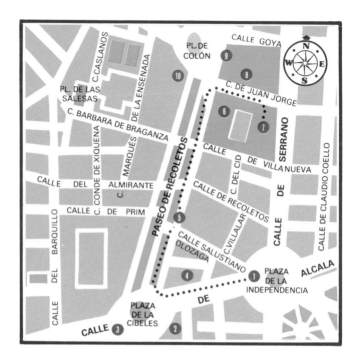

ALONG THE PASEO DE RECOLETOS

1. Plaza de la Independencia
2. Palacio de Comunicaciones
3. Banco de España
4. Palacio de Linares
5. Palacio del Marqués de Salamanca
6. Biblioteca Nacional
7. Museo Nacional Arqueológico
8. Jardines del Descubrimiento
9. Centro Cultural de la Villa
10. Museo de Cera

of Spain), slightly less impressive than the building we have just seen. It was built in 1891, and has recently been enlarged without damaging its original style. Opposite the bank, again on Calle Alcalá, is the Army Administration building, once the **Buenavista Palace**. This palace, built of red brick and surrounded by parks and gardens, was built at the end of the 18th century as the permanent residence of the Duchess Cayetana of Alba. She died before construction was completed, and the palace changed hands several times before being taken over by the army.

Behind us now is the **Palacio de Linares**.

Regrettably, this lovely late 19th century palace is now deserted and neglected, and the *Madrileños* have successfully attached some fine ghost stories to it. And indeed, at certain times of the day, if you are in a particular mood, it can be a rather frightening place. Going a bit further, we reach the **Paseo de Recoletos** (Recoletos Promenade), whose name refers to the "Monastery of the Confined Monks" which used to stand here and whose superb wines were known far and wide. The Monastery was destroyed, and a fine palace built in its place – the **Palacio del Marqués de Salamanca** (Duke of Salamanca Palace). The story of his trouble-ridden life could fill several tomes. We mention only that he conspired, traded, collected, built, involved himself in politics and commerce. In other words, he had a hand in everything: banking, the Bourse, trains, communications, theater, circuses and much else. He was patron of many artists, and the richest man in the kingdom honored him by building a residential district bearing his name. In 1883 the Duke died penniless in his palace, leaving behind him countless debts. His palace, which was built in 1858, was a model much copied at the time. It is closed to the public.

We shall carry on along the same sidewalk. Between Calles Villanueva and Juan Jorge there is a building, both massive and elegant, of neo-classical lines. This is the

Paseo de Recoletos promenade

The Duke of Salamanca Palace in the Recoletos Promenade

Biblioteca Nacional (National Library). It was opened in 1892, the year celebrating the 400th year of the discovery of America. It is the most important library in Spain, containing more than five million books, including rare manuscripts from all over the world. The southern entrance leads to the exhibition hall, which displays exhibits on various subjects. The rare manuscripts are displayed on the second floor.

The neo-classical, powerful façade of the National Library

We walk around to the other side of the building, where we find the **Museo Nacional Arqueológico** (National Museum of Archeology), at 13 Calle Serrano. Open Tues.-Sat. 9:30am-8:30pm; Sun. 9:30am-2:30pm. Closed Mon. and public holidays. Entrance fee. Tel. 577-7912. The museum has a large collection of original artifacts which document the history of the Iberian Peninsula throughout the ages. In the museum's courtyard there is an exact replica of the Altamira Cave with its paleolithic drawings. This replica is particularly important since the actual cave is closed to visitors due to its poor condition.

Between Calles Goya, Serrano and Juan Jorge are the **Jardines del Descubrimiento** (Discovery of America Gardens). To their eastern side there are some sculpted blocks of concrete, meant to represent the journeys of Columbus to the new continent. On the southwestern side of the square is a statue in honor of the explorer. Below the square, at the foot of an extremely noisy waterfall, is the city's cultural center – **Centro Cultural de la Villa** – which houses theaters and exhibitions. The Discovery of America Gardens complex was and still is much criticized by the citizens of Madrid, who are not enamoured by the cold concrete square with its graceless blocks in the background. Even the statue of Columbus, which was erected in 1885, is not particularly liked, but the abundant waters of the fountain add some charm to the cold stone.

On the left sidewalk of Plaza de Colón, at 41 Paseo de Recoletos, is the **Centro Colón** (Columbus Center), with the **Museo de Cera** (Wax Museum). The museum contains wax models of important people from all periods of history and from all walks of life, as well as the popular "Chamber of Horrors". (Open every day, 10:30am-2pm and 4-9pm. Tel. 419-2649). Audio-visual shows are held at the Columbus Center, depicting the history of Spain in music and pictures.

The citizens often sit on the terraces of the Recoletos Promenade during the summer evenings, where the café proprietors put out tables. There are two especially good cafés on the western sidewalk. The most famous of all is the *Café Gijón*, at no. 21, where artists gather. This place has scarcely changed in the last 50 years, and has a warm and comfortable atmosphere. At no. 31 is *El Espejo*, decorated in the Art Nouveau style with taste and charm. At either of these places we can rest before our next tour.

The sculpted blocks in the Jardines del Descubrimiento

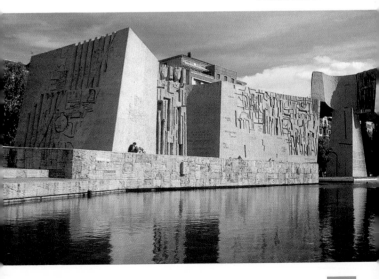

Plaza de Colón – named after Christopher Columbus

Other Places of Interest

Further along the Recoletos Promenade, past **Plaza de Colón** (Columbus Square), is **La Castellana Promenade**, which has become a prominent commercial center. Both sides of the street have modern new buildings. This quarter is the home of a number of foreign embassies. At the corner of Calles La Castellana and Juan Bravo, on the underpass, there is a sculpture garden, which displays the works of Spain's best contemporary sculptors, including among others Joan Miró, Chillada and Julio Gonzalez.

The street which runs parallel to the Recoletos and La Castellana Promenades is Calle Serrano – a main artery of the exclusive Salamanca district. There are lots of fine – and very expensive – stores here. Even more exclusive fashions can be found in Calle Almirante (see "Two Faces of Madrid").

At 122 Serrano you will find another interesting museum, *Lázaro Galdiano*, which houses a unique display of Goya and Velázquez paintings, as well as jewelry, ceramics and ivory. Open Tues.-Sun. 10am-2pm; closed Mon. Tel. 561-6084.

The spacious Recoletos Promenade

Two Faces of Madrid

Metro: Colón, Line 4
Buses: 5, 14, 21, 27, M-6, M-12.

This tour starts in **Plaza de Colón**. We turn into Calle Génova and walk as far as Calle General Castaños, where we turn left. On our left is **Plaza de la Villa de París**, a quiet place, now a relic of a grand park which was part of a complex which included a palace, a convent and a church. Queen Bárbara de Braganza, who feared for her fate should her husband, King Fernando VI, die before her and leave her alone in a stormy political sea, wanted to prepare herself a safe haven. She therefore founded the **Iglesia de las Salesas Reales**, where she planned to retire when the time came. Work on the plan continued for eight years and cost a fortune, which caused fierce criticism. The most popular song of the day was: "Barbaric expense, barbaric budget, barbaric people, Queen Bárbara". (It rhymes in Spanish!). Construction was finished in 1758, but the queen did not live to enjoy it – she died a few months before her husband. The church is one of the most magnificent in Madrid.

Its style is very French and baroque, weighed down with ornamentation. On either side of the main altar are two graves – on the right, that of Fernando VI, decorated with allegorical statues, and on the left that of General O'Donnell, hero of the African war. Scenes from the war are depicted on the tombstone on his grave.

In 1870 it was decided to move the nuns of the Convent to another place, and the building became the Ministry of Justice. It faces Calle Marques de la Ensenada, and opposite is an Art Nouveau building decorated with elephant heads.

The façade of Iglesia de las Salesas Reales, today serves as the Ministry of Justice

This was built in 1902 as a theater, it then became the French Institute, and is now empty, awaiting its next designation. At no. 17 on this street is the café and discotheque Bocaccio particularly liked by the cinema, theater and journalism crowd as well as by the city's beautiful people.

We now turn right into Calle Almirante, with its shops that ordinary mortals can only look at from the outside – these are the fashion outlets of Spain's most prestigious designers. Before becoming embittered at this social injustice, we had better turn into Calle Barquillo, the main thoroughfare of the Salesas district, where royal carriages used to pass on their way to church. There are still some lovely houses here, between the banks and the offices. This street is also

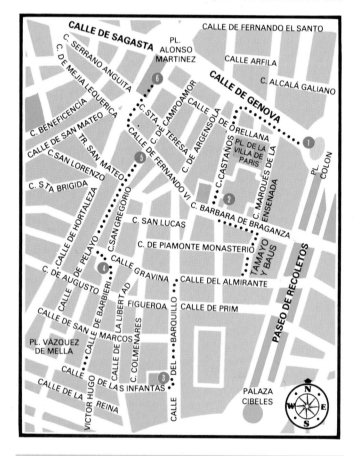

FROM PLAZA DE COLÓN TO PLAZA DE SANTA BÁRBARA

1. Plaza de Colón
2. Iglesia de las Salesas Reales
3. La Casa de las Siete Chimeneas
4. Plaza de Chueca
5. Casa Longoria
6. Plaza de Santa Bárbara

a kind of border crossing between two districts of different and contrasting character: on the left, aristocratic Salesas, while on the right, the very ordinary Chueca. We are still on the more elegant side, and leave it at the corner of Calles Barquillo and Infantas, on which stands one of the oldest houses in the city – **La Casa de las Siete Chimeneas** (House of the Seven Chimneys). It was built in 1577 and bought by a wealthy Italian banker, and has since changed hands many times. Its most famous owner was the Marquis of Esquilice, one of Carlos III's ministers. There are countless stories about the house. One tells of a woman who wanders through it at night bearing a torch, and legend has it that she was perhaps a princess who strayed from the straight and narrow and was imprisoned here, as the seven chimneys clearly symbolize the seven deadly sins. Some years ago, when work was being done on the building, a woman's skeleton was discovered, together with some coins from the time of Philip II. Today the building is part of the Ministry of Culture.

The rich ornamentation of the main altar in the Iglesia de las Salesas Reales

We now go along Calle Infantas, and soon feel that we have indeed crossed the border we spoke of earlier. We are in the *Chisperos* District – the name given at the time to those who worked in the many metal workshops that used to be here. They were poor and miserable people, and this was one of the first places to ignite at times of social agitation. Turning right into Calle Barbieri, we walk to the central square of the Chueca district. Don't look for monuments here.

Plaza de Santa Bárbara in the Chueca district

La Casa de las Siete Chimeneas – the seven chimneys symbolize the seven deadly sins

Everything is on a small and modest scale – the cafés and restaurants – even the square itself is not much more than a courtyard. At night it changes – the intimate warmth felt during the day vanishes, and the district turns into a meeting place for all sorts of savory and unsavory characters.

Continuing on along Calle Pelayo, we arrive at the corner of Calle Fernando VI. Here there is a lovely building, the **Casa Longoria**, which is today the home of the Union of Writers. It was built in 1902 in Art-Nouveau or Modernismo style. There are very few buildings in Madrid in this style, which blossomed more fully in Barcelona, where the architectural genius Antonio Gaudí worked, bringing the style to new heights. The style's characteristics are rounded, assymetric lines, closely-packed ornamentation and a combination of materials (stone, glass, ceramics, etc.). If the house is open,

it's worthwhile going in to see the beautiful staircase and the colored glass windows.

We turn left into Calle Fernando VI, and find ourselves in **Plaza de Santa Bárbara** – a very pleasant place to relax with terraces, cafés and restaurants and a youthful atmosphere.

Casa Longoria

Romantic Madrid

Metro: Alonso Martinez, Lines 4, 5, 10.
Buses: 3, 21.

We leave Plaza de Santa Bárbara via Calle San Mateo. At no. 13 is the **Museo Romántico** (Museum of Romance). Open Tues.-Sat. 9am-3pm, Sun. and holidays 9am-2pm. Closed Mon. and throughout August. Entrance fee. This lovely house was built in the 18th century by the disciple and relative of the famous Ventura Rodriguez. We can see the furniture, musical instruments, porcelain, ceramics, models of the salons in which meetings were held, a table laid, and even the bathroom – all once belonging to King Fernando VII. All these serve to make real for us the life-style of the period. Also in the museum is an interesting collection which includes paintings by Zurbarán, Goya and others.

We continue along Calle San Mateo to the noisy and packed Calle Fuencarral. Here we turn right and immediately see the exceptionally ornamented gate of the **Museo Municipal** (Municipal Museum). Open Tues.-Fri. 9am-9pm, Sat. and Sun. 9am-2pm. Closed on Mon. and holidays. Free entrance. Tel 542-5512. This building, designed by architects Pedro de Ribera and Churriguera, was erected in 1799, and was originally an orphanage and poorhouse. The museum houses exhibits displaying the history of the city, paintings, porcelain and photographs, and an archeology wing has recently been opened.

The ornamented gate of the Municipal Museum

Now we shall cross Calle Fuencarral and enter a new district via Calle Velarde. Once it was called Maravillas, which means "marvels", but today it is called Malasaña. Hashish is freely available here, and don't be surprised if at every corner you are offered "chocolate". Until a few decades ago, this

In the Municipal Museum, a display of furniture and porcelain from the history of the city

was a petit bourgeois district whose residents owned workshops; there were small traders, students and seamstresses. Over the years, the young men left the district, leaving behind shabby buildings and old people. Contractors slowly took an interest in the area, foreseeing the huge profits which could be made. They suggested pulling down the old houses and building a modern center, in finest concrete, metal and glass. However, the elderly residents, supported by thousands of young artists who cared, objected actively to the plan and brought new life to the area. Bars, pubs and restaurants mushroomed and burgeoned, and the district became a center for nightlife. You can find everything here: art deco cafés with "serious" music, post-modern grays and neon lighting, punk, and more – each in finest battle colors. All this happens at night. During the day, Malasaña is a quiet neighborhood where well-padded ladies traverse the streets on their daily round between the grocer and the butcher. This odd coexistence has been going on for years, to the satisfaction of all who abide there.

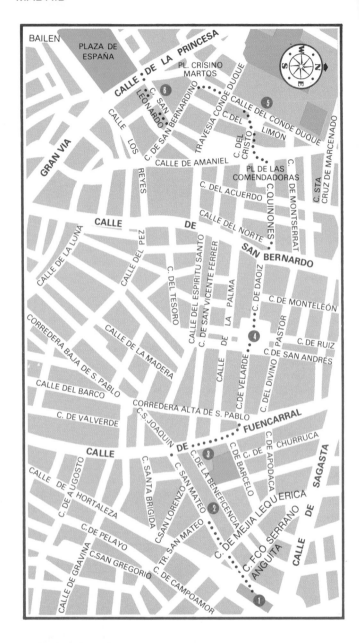

FROM PLAZA DE SANTA BÁRBARA TO TORRE DE MADRID

1. Plaza de Santa Bárbara
2. Museo Romántico
3. Museo Municipal
4. Plaza del Dos de Mayo
5. Cuartel del Conde Duque
6. Iglesia de San Marcos

Plaza del Dos de Mayo, commemorating the events of May 2, 1808

Back on Calle Velarde, we walk along to the heart and vital soul of the district – **Plaza del Dos de Mayo** (May 2 Square). The name refers to May 2, 1808, when people from all over the city gathered here and demanded arms to fight the French. Two young boys, Daoíz and Velarde, led the revolt, barricading themselves in for several hours. Finally, the French took the square after a fierce and bloody battle in which many lost their lives. The statue under the gate shows Daoíz and Velarde as they vow to fight to the end. The district's name is also connected with this revolt: a brave young girl named Manuela Malasaña was also one of its leaders, and was killed during the battle.

The ellipses at the Iglesia de San Marcos

Having reached the square via Calle Velarde, we shall leave by its companion, Calle Daoíz and walk to Calle San Bernardo. Turning right, we can see the **Iglesia de Montserrat**, whose interesting façade is the work of Pedro de Rivera. Crossing San Bernardo, we enter Calle Quiñones, and continue along it as far as the Plaza de las Comendadoras, which contains the **Iglesia de las Comendadoras de Santiago**. The church was built in 1675, and is older than the monastery (it is currently closed to the public). Nearby are barracks – **Cuartel del Conde Duque**. The history of this site begins in 1704, when King Philip V reorganized the army and created a corps to

act as the king's bodyguard – the *Guardias de Corps*. One of its members was a man named Godoy, who watched closely over the king, while at the same time the queen watched closely over him, and made him one of the most powerful men of his time. The architect of the baroque façade of the building is Pedro de Ribera. The barracks has recently been cleaned and renovated, and there is a small park next to it, which holds exhibitions and stages plays.

Continue along Conde Duque to San Bernardo, and turn right into Calle San Leonardo, and stop outside the **Iglesia de San Marcos**. This is an interesting church, designed by the great Ventura Rodriguez. There are no straight lines inside the church, and it is in fact based on five unequal ellipses. St. Mark sits on a lion at the main altar. Since the lion is associated with the saint, it appears in several places in the church. Outside the church, a few steps further on, is the **Plaza de España**. This is a huge and charmless square, with the bombastic and pretentious statue of Cervantes at its center and Don Quixote and Sancho Panza next to it. At the southern end of the square, in Calle Bailén, there is a very fine building, the **Compañía Asturiana de Minas**, founded in 1896. On the same side of the square there is a neo-Gothic building with a ceramic-covered dome in bold colors. This was built in 1923 as the Santa Teresa Convent. Now look in the western corner of Plaza de España and Calle Ferraz, where there is a lovely apartment house built in the twenties. Opposite us is the Edificio España, erected in 1948, combining traditional elements with new building

Torre de Madrid catches your eye as you exit the Plaza de España

techniques. Finally, there is the **Torre de Madrid** (Madrid Tower), which was for years the highest building in the capital. On its 32nd floor there is a café, *Casa de Cantabria*, which is also a meeting place for people from that region. We can end our tour here, looking out over the city from this great height. Entrance fee 50 pesetas, closed Sun.

Plaza de España, next to the Church of San Marcos

Nature and Art

Metro: Plaza de España, Line 3, 10.
Buses: 1, 2, 39, 44, Circular, M-5, M-8.

Our starting point is the corner of **Plaza de España** and Calle Ferraz. Our first stop is almost at our starting point. At the corner of Calle Ferraz and Calle Ventura Rodriguez is a museum: **Museo Cerralbo**. This museum is actually a private palace housing many collections, which were donated to the state by its owner, the Marquis of Cerralbo. Built in 1884, the building contains collections of paintings, porcelain, tapestries and ancient weapons. The paintings include works by El Greco, Zurbarán, Goya, Murillo, Tiepolo and others. In addition to all these, the house gives the visitor some inkling of the life of the Spanish aristocracy in the last century. At the time of writing, the museum is closed to the public. For details regarding its opening call: Tel. 547-3646.

In Plaza de España – Cervantes alongside his heroes, Don Quixote and Sancho Panza

Back in Calle Ferraz, we cross the road, to a grassy hill and gardens: these are the **Jardines Cuartel de la Montaña** (Barracks Hill Gardens). There was a barracks here once, whose soldiers joined the nationalist uprising in 1936. The barracks was destroyed when the people of Madrid took the hill. The monument at the entrance to the park was erected in Franco's time. Another historical event took place here: the executions of the rebels who, on May 2, 1808, faced Napoleon's army almost unarmed.

They are buried not far from here, and the executions were commemorated by Goya in two paintings – *The March on the Second of May 1808*, *The Executions on the Third of May* – which are displayed in the Prado.

The Egyptians presented this shrine to the Spanish government

We climb to the top of the hill where a surprise awaits us – the building on the quiet waters of the small cistern that looks like, and is in fact, an **ancient Egyptian shrine**. In 1970, the Egyptian government gave the shrine to the government of Spain, in gratitude to the delegation of Spanish archeologists, under the aegis of UNESCO, who had helped save the architectural complex at Nubia, which is a shrine to the god Ammon dating from the fourth century BC. From the observation points around the shrine, you can look out over the city. This unusual site is highly recommended.

Ermita de la Florida – here Goya is buried

We now continue along the **Paseo de Pintor Rosales**, built after the Civil War. Previously, this was an upper bourgeois district, and today is still considered quite high class. Although close to the city center, it is quiet and green. Opposite the **Parque del Oeste** (Western Park), *Madrileños* like to sit on the sidewalk and have a drink, breathe the air and enjoy all the greenery. The lovely large park is not very popular with the locals, who prefer to throng to the Retiro. We go into the park from the steep Calle Francisco y Jacinto Alcántara, alongside the train which goes to Casa de Campo. On our way down we pass the Rosaleda (Rose Garden), next to the State School for ceramics and a small cemetery – Cementerio de la Florida, where the heroes of May 2 are buried.

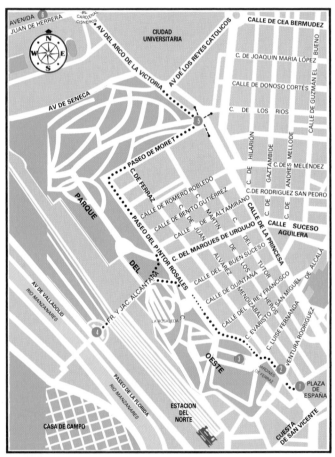

ALONG PARQUE DEL OESTE

1. Plaza de España
2. Museo Cerralbo
3. Egyptian Shrine (El Templo de Debod)
4. Ermita de la Florida
5. Moncloa Complex
6. Museo de Arte Contemporáneo

We continue on to the Paseo de la Florida, where we can see the church of the **Ermita de la Florida**. In fact there are two hermitages, one genuine and one a copy. We shall visit the real one, which is the more southerly. The original one, containing the mausoleum of Goya, and his wonderful tapestries, has become an artistic monument. It was built in 1797. For 120 days Goya worked on the the superb roof and wall-paintings depicting one of St. Antony's miracles before the onlookers. He painted ordinary people of his time, beggars, the sick, and common people, crowding round the circular balustrade. The almost expressionist style, so long before its time, is very clear here. Goya's grave is also to be found here. The church is dedicated to St. Antony, who has the power – so believers will tell you – to obtain a husband for even the most unlikely of candidates. Every year in June, a festival is held in honor of St. Antony – June is when he can help the most. The saint himself is helped by the drinking and dancing and general gaiety which are part of the happening. In order to accommodate both believers and art-lovers, the shrine was duplicated.

A statue of one of Spain's most famous artists, Francisco Goya

Opposite the shrines there is a charming bridge over the Mensanares. On the left there is a large restaurant – *Casa Mingo* – with good plain food: roast chicken, cider and cheeses. The restaurant is a relic of the time when the banks of the Mensanares were lined with eating places patronized by the *Madrileños*.

Let's go back to the Parque del Oeste and walk around for a while, slowly winding our way back to the street from which we came – Calle Pintor Rosales. We then continue to the end, and turn right into Paseo de Moret. We continue straight on until we reach the **Moncloa Complex**. Here you can clearly see the connection between ideology and architecture. This is a clear example of Fascist architecture. It is well known that the

Moncloa Complex was overseen by Hitler's architect, Albert Speer. The complex is made up of three buildings: Ministerio del Aire (the Air Force Administration), the Plus Ultra Monument and the **Arco de Triunfo** (Victory Gate). The **Ministerio del Aire** was built between 1942-1951. The alternating use of red brick and stone is well known to us from many buildings of the Hapsburg period. The Plus Ultra Monument was dedicated to men of the Nationalist Army who fell in the Civil War. Completing the complex is the massive Arco de Triunfo. Beneath the four horses which crown it is a Latin inscription glorifying Franco's military victory.

To our right is the Madrid University campus. Continuing along Avenida Arco de la Victoria we come to Plaza Grutal del Cardinal Cisneros, and turn right at Avenida Juan de Herrera. In this street, at No. 2, there is a new and harmoniously designed building – Museo de Arte Contemporáneo (Museum of Contemporary Art). It was built in 1965 and won an important architectural award. It houses works by the greatest of Spanish contemporary artists, such as Picasso, Miro, and Dali. (Open Tues.– Sat. 10am-6pm; Sun. 10am-3pm. Closed on Monday and holidays.).

A massive structure, one of the three buildings that comprise the Moncloa Complex

EXCURSIONS

In this chapter we will suggest some places beyond the city's limits – yet nearby – that are well worth a visit. Public transport to all these places is convenient. The Spanish Railway Authority (*Renfe*) organizes guided tours to some of these locations during May-October. For information refer to any travel agency, or call Tel. 530-0202. You can also call Tel. 401-9900 (bus), and 435-2266 (metro).

El Pardo

In 1405 this spot had already been chosen as the site of the Royal Palace. Enrique III chose it, for the abundant hunting possibilities in the vicinity. Since then, the royal grounds have expanded, and today they include enormous tracts of woodland. You can visit the church, the Prince's Residence, the Farm and the Zarzuela Palace, three miles from El Pardo, where the royal family now lives. A tour of the Pardo is a tour through breathtaking scenery and beautiful palaces. *Madrileños* often come here on holidays, to dine at the numerous restaurants.

PALACIO DE EL PARDO

Charles I was responsible for the building of the palace. It was burned down in 1605, and of the original structure only the tower and the western gate remain. The extensions to the old building are the work of the architect Sabatini, a contemporary of King Charles III. Retaining the original style, Sabatini added the many chimneys and the interesting apertures in the towers. The

tapestries are worthy of special mention, copied from paintings by Goya. During the Civil War, the International Brigades were billetted in the building, and from 1940, General Franco lived here. Next to the palace there is a church, which was built in

1783 in classical style. The exterior combines brick and flint pillars; inside, there are paintings by Lucas Jordán, and a large painting of "The Immaculate Virgin" (*La Inmaculada*) by Maella. Open daily 10am-1pm and 3:30-6pm.

CASITA DEL PRINCIPE (THE PRINCE'S RESIDENCE)

This is a lovely building, dating from 1785, which was built by the "Escorial" architect, Juan de Vianueva. In contrast to its classical exterior, the interior excels in splendor: works in gilded plaster, marble and velvet cover the walls and ceilings; paintings adorn the halls. Open daily 10am-1pm and 4-7pm, holidays 10am-1pm.

LA QUINTA (THE FARM)

Today a museum, this was originally a summer-house given as a gift to King Philip V. An archway of brick and stone is the entrance to the garden, with its numerous statues, fountains, caves and terraces. Inside there is an interesting collection of colored paper – imitation felt in the style popular in France at the end of the 18th century. Open daily 10am-1pm and 3:30-6pm.

Aranjuez is known for its beautiful gardens

How to get there: Buses – from Paseo Moret (Metro – Moncloa).

Alcalá de Henares

This town is 20 miles from Madrid and is a pleasant surprise for the visitor. It has a long cultural tradition. In 1496, a university was founded here; the beautiful building has been preserved to this day, although the university was moved to Madrid in 1836 and the *Paraninfo* (Central Hall) is particularly recommended. There is a lovely church nearby, the *Iglesia Magistral*, and also the Palacio Arzobispal (Bishop's Palace). Here, at Calle Mayor 48, you can also visit **Casa de Cervantes**, the house where the great writer Cervantes was born in 1547. This house is now a museum.

Tourist information center: Callejón de Santa María, Tel. 889-2694.

How to get there: Trains – from Atocha and Chamartín stations every 30 minutes; Buses – from 18 Avenida de América every 15 minutes (Metro América). By car – N11 from Barcelona.

Aranjuez – serenity reigns supreme

Aranjuez

Thirty miles from Madrid, this town is on the Andelusia road. Its special beauty is the subject of the famous "Concerto Aranjuez" by Joaquim Rodrigo. There are two sites worth visiting here. One is the **Palacio Real** (Royal Palace), which was the Bourbon monarchs' summer home in the eighteenth century, with its lovely gardens, next to the River Tagus. The other is the **Casa del Labrador** (Farmer's House), with its collection of porcelain objects and old clocks. The house was built on a model of the Royal Palace and is surrounded by woodland and gardens, waterfalls and tranquil lakes. Tourist services in Aranjuez are of a high standard, and there are numerous restaurants on the banks of the Tagus. Don't miss

Aranjuez

Aranjuez's famous strawberries and asparagus.

Tourist information center: Plaza de Santiago Rusiñol, Tel. 891-0427.

How to get there: Trains – from Atocha station; buses – from Sur station, 17 Calle Canarias (Metro – Palos de Moguer). By car – NIV to Andalusia.

El Escorial

This site is 31 miles from Madrid, and its attraction lies in its natural beauty. Here too is one of the most important buildings in Spain – the famous and unparalleled monastery-palace built by the architect Juan de Herrera. Open Apr. 15 – Sept. 15, 10am-1pm and 3-7pm; Sept. 15 – Apr. 15, 10am-1pm and 3-6pm; closed Mon. This imposing building was built by Philip II, who personally supervised its construction. It has a grandiose austerity even though it has over 2,000 windows. There is a very good slide show, with optional English commentary on the age of Philip II.

Royal apartments or **Palacios** occupy a quarter of the building. Some of the sumptuous 300 tapestries which cover the walls of

the Palace have been copied from drawings by Goya. Philip II's apartments on the second floor are striking in their austerity. Here Philip II died in 1598 when he was 71. The **Church** built in the shape of a Greek cross is dedicated to St. Peter. The huge dome is supported by four enormous central pillars. The red marble columns which surround the altar are also the work of Herrara. The **Royal Pantheon** has 26 identical sarcophagi in baroque style. Most of the Spanish kings since Charles I are buried here. The palace is a treasure-house of works of art and manuscripts.

Valle de Los Caidos

Apart from the monastery-palace, a visit to the Casita del Príncipe (Prince's Residence) is also recommended. This graceful pavilion was built during the reign of Charles III for the future Charles IV, the Asturies prince.

Tourist information center: 10 Floridablanca, Tel. 890-1554.

How to get there: Trains – from Atocha,

Chamartín and Norte-Principé Pio stations; buses – from 10 Isaac Peral (Metro – Moncloa). By car – N-VI (leading to La Coruña); exit Las Rozas.

VALLE DE LOS CAIDOS (VALLEY OF THE WAR DEAD)

This site is not far from El Escorial, in a wild valley stretching along the foot of the Guadarrama range. The monument was erected to honor the dead Francoists. The Basilica itself was carved by republican prisoners and General Franco is buried in the crypt with 400 soldiers. The gigantic cross (500ft. high, 150ft. wide) is made of silica. You can reach it by cablecar, otherwise it's rather tricky to get to.

How to get there: Buses – from El Escorial.

Toledo

A journey of about 50 miles brings us to Toledo – the emperors' capital until 1561. We are welcomed by a gate called *La Puerta de Bisagra*, which carries the shield of Carlos V. Behind it lies a fascinating world. Under the Moors (712-1085) and the kings of Castile, Toledo was a center of Moorish, Spanish and Jewish culture, and it was noted for its sword blades and textiles. In the 16th century it was the seat of the Spanish Inquisition. There are many superb buildings which convey something of the culture which thrived here centuries ago. Here you can see the Gothic cathedral, the Jewish Quarter with its synagogues, and the churches and mosques.

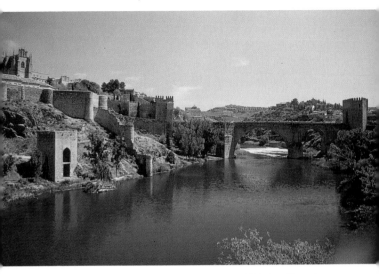

El Greco, the Greek painter, lived and worked in the royal city of Toledo when it was the capital of Spain. The artist's house, **Casa y Museo de El Greco** should not be missed. Open: Tues.-Sat. 10am-2pm and 4-6pm; Sun. 10am-2pm. Closed Mon. It contains some of his personal objects, some lovely paintings, such as the *Penitent St. Peter*, and a series of Jesus and the Apostles. More of his works can be seen in the cathedral, the Hospital of San Juan Bautista and the Iglesia de Santo Tome.

The imposing cathedral in Toledo is a mixture of French and Spanish styles and is one of the most impressive in Spain. It has eight doors, three of which stand in the main façade. The inside is divided into 20 chapels which have works by Goya, El Greco and a few from the Flemish school. The Mozarabic chapel, built on the orders of Cardinal Cisneros, still celebrates mass according to Mozarbic ritual. In the chapter house you'll notice magnificent ceilings with Mudejar colorings.

Toledo had eight synagogues in the Middle Ages but at the time of the eviction of the

Toledo still retains medieval charm

Segovia – the Alcázar

Jews from Spain, most of them were destroyed or transformed into churches. For example, the **Sinagoga del Transito** offers remarkable Mudejar decorations and a museum on Spanish Jewish culture. The **Sinagoga de Santa Maria la Blanca**, Toledo's principal synagogue, was transformed into a church in 1405 on the orders of Calatrava, who gave it his name. It is sculpted in Andalusian style.

If you really want to catch the atmosphere of Toledo, we recommend that you walk through the narrow winding streets alongside the River Tagus.

Tourist information center: Puerta de Bisagra, s/n, Tel. (925)220-843.

How to get there: Trains – from Atocha station; buses – from Sur station, 17 Canarias (Metro – Palos de Moguer). By car – N-401.

Segovia

This is an ancient Roman city whose most familiar landmark is its enormous aqueduct (10 miles long). There is a very impressive 16th century Gothic cathedral in Segovia, as well as other interesting churches such as the San Milan church (12th century). From the Alcázar you can look out over a beautiful landscape. Not far from the city are the Granja de San Idelfonso palace and gardens, which were ordered by Philip V, and have a touch of nostalgia for Versailles. Recommended.

Tourist information center: 10 Plaza Mayor, Tel. (911)430-328.

How to get there: Trains – from Atocha station; buses – from 11 Paseo de la Florida (Metro – Norte). By car – N-601.

Chinchón

To the south of the Madrid district, 35 miles away, you will find the medieval town of Chinchón. Plaza Mayor, the wooden houses, the church and the Gothic castle are all worth a visit. Bullfights take place in season. It is also known for its good food and *anis*, distilled in the castle, which you really shouldn't miss.

How to get there: Buses – from 7 Sanchez Bustillo (Metro – Atocha). By car – N-111 to Valencia; turn right at Arganda Bridge.

A panoramic view of Toledo

MUSTS

For those of you who only have a short time and cannot possibly take all the tours, we have prepared a list of locations without which a visit to Madrid is not really complete.

PALACIO REAL DE ORIENTE

A magnificent palace on the site of the former Alcázar Fortress. Inside the building is a dazzling collection of art, furniture, tapestries and statues (see "To the Palace!").

Buses: Circular, 25, 33, 36, 41 and 50.

MUSEO DEL PRADO

A world famous museum, containing a superb collection of paintings, sculpture and jewelry (see "The Prado Museum and the Retiro Gardens").

Metro: Banco, line 2. Buses 10, 14, 27, M6.

PLAZA MAYOR

The main square of the city, still has an atmosphere of another era. Performances are held here in summer, but a good place to visit at any time (see "Ancient Madrid").

Museo del Prado houses an amazing art collection

Metro: Sol, lines 1, 2, 3. Buses: 5, 15, 17, 20, 23, 50, 51, 52, 53.

Magnificent gardens of the Palacio Real de Oriente

PLAZA DE LA VILLA
An elegant peaceful square surrounded by lovely historic buildings (see "Ancient Madrid").

Metro: Sol, lines 1, 2, 3. Buses: 5, 15, 17, 20, 23, 50, 51, 52, 53.

PLAZA DE LA CIBELES
A square with a fountain and statues carved by artists from many different countries. Surrounded by monumental buildings (see "Along the Paseo de Recoletos").

Metro: Retiro, line 2. Buses: 15, 28, M-2, M-8.

Plaza de la Cibeles

CONVENTO DE LAS DESCALZAS REALES
Established in the 16th century, it contains a wonderful collection of art (see "Spiritual Madrid").

Metro: Opera, lines 2, 5. Buses: 25, 33, 39.

PUERTA DE ALCALÁ
Historic entrance to the city near the impressive Plaza de la Independencia (see "Along the Paseo de Recoletos").

Metro: Retiro, line 2. Buses: 15, 28, M-2, M-8.

Highly Recommended

Once a home for orphans, today the Municipal Museum displays the city's history

CATEDRAL DE SAN ISIDRO
Built in the 17th century by the Jesuit Order, and later adapted as a Royal Church (see "From Plaza de Neptuno to the "Low Districts"").

Buses: 27, 34, 14, M-6.

BASÍLICA DE SAN MIGUEL
A beautiful 18th century church in Italian baroque style (see "Ancient Madrid").

Metro: Sol, lines 1, 2, 3. Buses: 5, 15, 17, 20, 23, 51, 52, 53.

IGLESIA DE SAN MARCOS
Fascinating architecture by Ventura Rodriguez (see "Romantic Madrid").

Metro: Alonso Martinez, lines 4, 5, 10. Buses: 3, 21.

IGLESIA DE LAS COMENDADORAS DE SANTIAGO
The beautiful baroque church was built in 1675. Named for Santiago, who led Spain to victory over the Moors (see "Romantic Madrid").

Metro: Alonso Martinez, lines 4, 5, 10. Buses 3, 21.

ATOCHA RAILWAY STATION
A handsome art nouveau building. (see "Arts and sciences – From Plaza de Lavapiés to the Botanical Gardens").

Metro: Lavapiés, line 3.

Atocha Railway station

PALACIO DE COMUNICACIONES
Astounding eclectic combination of architectural styles (see "Along the Paseo de Recoletos").

Metro: Retiro, line 2. Buses: 15, 28, M-2, M-8.

MUSEO MUNICIPAL
Displays the history of the city, paintings, porcelain, photographs and archeology (see "Romantic Madrid").

Metro: Alonso Martinez, lines 4, 5, 10. Buses 3, 21.

MUSEO ESPAÑOL DE ARTE CONTEMPORÁNEO
Contains works by the greatest modern Spanish artists, including Picasso, Miro and Dali (see "Nature and Art").

Metro: Plaza Española, lines 3, 10. Buses: 1, 2, 39, 44, Circular, M-5, M-8.

Iglesia de San Marcos

MAKING THE MOST OF YOUR STAY

Wining and Dining

The Spanish are known for their love of food, drink and good conversation. This is apparent in the countless cafés, restaurants, bars and wine cellars of Madrid.

A gastronomical delight – just around the corner

Knowing what you want isn't always so easy. Do you fancy a quiet corner for a conversation over a glass of wine? Or maybe somewhere noisy, where you can munch on some interesting snacks with your wine? Each has its time and place. The Spanish rule is: Finished your meal? Your drink? Then let's move on – we may be missing something round the corner!

The Spanish gastronomical daily schedule has laws of its own: at around 10am the sleepy Spaniard starts his day with a cup of good strong coffee and a glass of *Anisette* (a kind of Arak) or brandy. An alternative, especially in winter, is a cup of hot chocolate – a thick and somewhat startling drink – served with *churros*, which are long strips of fried dough. The more conventional way is coffee with milk, and croissants. Breakfast is obtainable at most cafes from about 7-11am. At 1pm the round of *tapas* (snacks) which are the hors d'oeuvres, begins with beer from the barrel or a good Spanish wine. The most popular snacks are snails (*gambas*), ham (*jamón*), local cheeses, and tiny river-fish either fried or pickled (*boquerones*), and there are many more. That's how it's done – going from one place to another, tasting a bit here, a bit there, until a decision can be reached as to the right place for lunch.

In Madrid you can find regional food from every corner of Spain, as well as restaurants which specialize in food from other countries. The typical dishes of the area are simple, but with an emphatic flavor. The most famous dish of all is the *cocido* – a simple stew containing chickpeas, vegetables, sausage and bits of pork, all generously peppered and spiced. A portion of that, together with some local wines, will brighten up the dullest winter day.

Another dish of similar qualities is beef, Madrid style (*callos a la Madrileña*). You can also eat Valencian paella in Madrid, shell-fish from Galicia, Andalusian gazpacho and wines from all over the country.

As you well know, "man does not live on bread alone". A place's character and design also contribute to the experience. Check the prices too – you will find them on a list posted either outside or just inside the restaurant.

After our first gastronomical tour, a rest of two or three hours is in order. Then, at about 5pm, everything starts anew: chocolate with *churros* and a round of the bars. From 10pm onwards it is the time to start looking for a place to have dinner. For the newcomers to such a regimen this may seem disastrous, but in fact one adjusts to it very quickly.

Restaurants

Here is a short list of restaurants. The first two appear in international gastronomy guides, and are rated among the best in the world. Bon appétit!

BASQUE

Príncipe de Viana: 5 Manuel de Falla, Tel. 457-1549. Closed Sat. lunch time, Sun. and from Jul. 15 to Sept.1.

Zalacaín: 4 Alvarez de Baena, Tel. 561-4840. Closed Sat. lunch time, Sun., holidays and throughout Aug.

El Amparo: 8 Callejón de Puigcerde, Tel. 431-6456. Closed Sat. lunch time, Sun., Easter week and throughout Aug.

CENTRAL EUROPEAN (VENISON)

Horcher: 6 Alfonso XII, Tel. 523-3490. Closed Sun.

CATALAN

El Bodegón: 15 Pinar, Tel. 562-8844. Closed Sun. and from Aug. 12-Sept. 22.

INTERNATIONAL (HAUTE CUISINE)

Club 31: 58 Alcala, Tel. 231-0092. Closed throughout Aug.

FISH AND SEAFOOD

El Pescador: 75 Jos, Ortega y Gasset, Tel. 401-3026. Closed Sun. and from Aug. 12 to Sept. 22.

VEGETARIAN FOOD

El Granero de Layapiés: 10 Argumosa. Lunch only. Closed Mon.
Arturo: 8 Plaza República Argentina, Tel. 411-3660. Closed Sun. and first two weeks of August.

GALICIAN

Cabo Mayor: 37 Juán Ramon Jiménez, Tel. 350-8776. Closed Sun. and throughout Aug.

Gure-Etxea: 12 Plaza de la Paja, Tel. 365-6149. Closed Sun. and throughout Aug.

FRENCH (HAUTE CUISINE)

Jockey: 6 Amador de los Rios,

Tel. 419-2435. Closed Sun. and throughout Aug.

ASADORES (ON THE GRILL)

Asador Frontón I: 7 Tirso de Molina, Tel. 369-1617. Closed Sun. and throughout Aug.

Asador Orio: 83 Paseo de la Castellana, Tel. 556-2291. Closed Sun. evenings.

Another list of restaurants follows, according to the type of food and its place of origin. They are rated according to the price range (in *pesetas*):

1) less than 1,500

2) 1,500-2,500
3) 2,500-3,500
4) 3,500-4,500
5) Over 4,500

Regional Specialities

Spanish cuisine is extremely varied and each region has its specialties. **Andalusía** specializes in gazpacho, paella and shellfish. You can taste *lubina al sal* (salt fish) and traditional fried fish. **Asturias** cuisine is a little like French cuisine. It offers a dish close to "cassoulet": the Fabada (pork meat with white beans) as well as a hot cheese: the *queso de cabrales*. **Basque** specialties are sauce dishes. Apart from those dishes, you can order *angulas* (fried eels) as well as *calamaras en su tinta* (calmars cooked in their ink). Restaurants specializing in **Castilian** cuisine will offer some *cochinillo asado* (roasted suckling pig) and excellent asparagus. **Catalan** cuisine

offers *Zarzuela de mariscos* (fish chowder), and meat dishes based on *jabali* (young wild boar), and on *cochinillo* (wild boar), everything well spiced with garlic. **Galicia's** specialties are cockles and shell-fish and the *empanadas*, puff-paste stuffed with meat or fish. **Valencia's** cuisine proposes the best paella, a dish eaten for lunch more commonly than for dinner.

ANDALUSIAN
Berrio: 4 Costanilla de Capuchinos, Tel. 521-2035. Closed Sun. (3).

Bocaito: 4-6 Libertad, Tel. 532-1219. Closed Sat. and Sun. (2).

BASQUE
El Espejo: 31 Paseo de Recoletos, Tel. 308-2347. (2).
Francisca: 14 Bailen, Tel. 265-1132. Closed Mon. (2)

A Madrid pub – anything from light rosé to the more potent Ribeiro

CASTILIAN
Sobrinos del Botín: 17 Cuchilleros, Tel. 266-4217. Closed Sun. (3).

Casa Paco: 11 Puerta Cerrada, Tel. 266-3166. (3).

La Quinta del Sordo: 10 Sacramento, Tel. 548-1852. Closed Sun. evenings. (2).

CATALAN
L'Emporda: 32 Comandante Zorita, Tel. 553-9342. Closed Sun. evenings. (3).

Paradis: 14 Marqués de Cubas, Tel 429-7303. Closed Sun., evenings and holidays.

GALICIAN
Bogavante: 20 Capitan Haya, Tel. 556-2114. Closed Sun. evenings. (3).

O'pazo: 20 Reina Mercedes, Tel. 553-2333. Closed Sun. (3).

ASTURIAS
Casa Portal: 26 Dr. Castelo, Tel. 574-2026. Closed Sun. (2).

Casa Mingo: 2 Paseo de la Florida, Tel 547-7918. (1).

Valle: 5 Ponciano, Tel. 541-5781. Closed Sun. evenings. (2).

VALENCIAN
La Barraca: 29 Reina, Tel. 532-7154.

Cheers!
If it is true that "a glass of wine is a glass of health", then the Spanish are one of the healthiest people in the world. Any opportunity is the right one for a toast, and not necessarily with wine: beer, gin, Anisette, brandy – all are equally suitable. We shall not tire you with details, or try to make you experts in this particular field! We shall merely

give some basic information about what to drink with your meal, and what to drink as an apéritif.

In 1979, the well-known monthly magazine *Gault et Millaut* organized a Wine Olympics in Paris, with the participation of 62 expert wine-tasters, who tasted 600 of the best wines in the world.

The results were quite surprising – the experts clearly preferred the wines of California, Catalonia and La Rioja – and no one argues with an expert.

We shall start with the wines from La Rioja – an area in north-west Spain with first-class vineyards. If you are having meat, ask for *Rioja tinto* (red wine), which will also smooth the way for heavier food.

The following is a list of very fine red wines, available at every restaurant:

San Asensio, Coto de Iniaz, Carta de Oro, Carta de Plata, Marqués de Riscal, Marqués de Cáceres.

If you are opting for a fish meal, or shellfish, ask for Galicia wine. The *Ribeiro*, which has a very delicate flavor, is served chilled in a white porcelain cup. Drink carefully – it's potent stuff

For those who find it hard to choose, we suggest a rosé wine, which goes with everything. A good rosé wine, as served in Spain, is always Catalonian. The Catalonian Torres Reserva is also good, but it is not available everywhere. But you can always ask the waiter for the house wine – *vino de la casa* – which is reasonably priced. These are usually from the Madrid area, and if not the very best, certainly satisfactory.

We must not forget Spanish sparkling wine – *cava*, from Catalonia –- which is a serious rival to the French variety because of its low price and fine taste. In 1983 Spain sold one hundred million bottles of *cava* around the world. There are a few places in Madrid where you can get the very best champagne, usually with the accompaniment of appropriate music. The best-known names are *Castellblanch, Seguravuidas, Freixenet* and *Codorniu.*

Madrileños are particularly fond of the following drinks, and we recommend that you try them too: *Sol y Sombra* (Sun and Shade), which is half Anisette, half brandy; *Carajillo* – warmed cognac with sugar, in boiling hot coffee; the perfect drink for a cold winter day. For the ladies, we recommend the Basque liqueur *Patzaran*, which has a superb sweet-and-sour taste (it's served with ice).

Sidra, a sparkling apple drink available from the barrel or in

bottles, should also be mentioned. There are two kinds: *Mastorias*, which is sweeter, and *Basque*, which is drier. *Sidra* should be poured from high above the glass, a little at a time, to improve the aeration.

The last name on the list is *Jeréz* or *Fino*, as they call it here. These are wines from southern Spain, very dry, with a very special taste. They are considered to be Spain's exhibition wines. The best known among them are *La Ina*, *Tío Pepe* and *Quinta*. Those who like sweet wines should ask for *Moscatel*, an unforgettable experience.

Entertainment

There is nowhere like Madrid at night – the streetlighting is barely lit when the air begins to tremble. Nightlife is what Madrid does better than most other cities – it's dynamic and fast-flowing. To discover it, just walk along the streets: no need to be afraid, it's what everybody else is doing too. Whether in a sumptuous nightclub or an old pub, you are likely to find bullfighters, computer programmers, university lecturers, factory workers, artists, and young girls wearing the shortest shorts you have ever seen. Everyone is there. Ask someone to direct you to the place you're looking for – and don't be afraid, they'll answer you and even help you look for it. Talk to people – there's nothing the *Madrileños* like better than to talk; it's a national sport. And meeting places for conversation, whether with friends or with strangers, are an "institution" here. Each citizen has his favorite bars, cafes and night-clubs. It's a city where a person spends most of his waking hours in the streets. The street in Madrid is not merely a means of getting from here to there; it's one of the most entertaining, amusing – and cheapest – places in the world.

We have divided the city into nine nightlife areas:

ARGUELLES – MONCLOA

This is a university district "par excellence", and therefore a favorite with the young, especially students. There are plenty of fast food places, hamburgers, pizzerias, pubs, discos, cafés and beer cellars.

The beer flows freely at *Parador de la Moncloa*, 2 Isaac Peral, and at *Cleo*, *Antoxo*, *El Masón del Marisco* and *Kebab House* (specializing in Lebanese-style snacks) – all in Calle Menéndez Valdés. If you want to go dancing, or to have a drink to the sound of music, try the exciting *Sky* at 7 Galileo, the quieter *Sándalo* at 2 Serrano Jover, or the *Delfín Piano Pub* on the same street. At *El Mississippi*, 45 Princesa, you can enjoy a dance hall with the atmosphere of a pub and beer house. At 47 Princesa you'll find *Bubu*, with the very latest in rhythm. Around Calles Adrés Mellado, Fernando el Católico, Meléndez Valdéz and Gaztambide there are about 50 places to have a good time among the buildings and court-yards. The *Parque del Oeste* is close by, a lovely park with many outdoor cafés in the vicinity, where you can have an ice-cream or beer, or just stroll about.

GRAN VÍA

All along this main street and in the streets adjacent to it there are nightclubs, restau-rants, cafés and striptease clubs. At 35-54 Gran Vía there are two of the city's best known night-clubs: *King Club* and *La Trompeta*. Nearby Leganitos is the center for the "Men Only" clubs, although there are others types of clubs here too. Plaza Callao is the address of *Xenon*, the famous music hall; and at 4 Calle Jacometrezo, you will find the *Oba-Oba* club with its Brazil-ian music. For those who like old-fashioned dancing, try the *Bali-Hai*, at 8 Flor Alta, or *La Carroza* at 4 Flor Baja. *Bar Chicote* is one of the places with the most deep-rooted tra-dition in Madrid, and is also recommended.

LAVAPIÉS – TIRSO DE MOLINA

This district, one of the oldest in Madrid, is now the theatrical center and favorite spot of Bohemians. The Olympian Theater, or the "The Center for New Directions in Theater", at Plaza de Lavapiés, has been joined by El Teatro del Mirador, (31 Dr. Fourquet), which is a puppet theater for both adults and children. There are old taverns here as well as new meeting places. *El Nuevo Café de Barbierei*, Plaza de Lavaliés, dates from the twenties, and today has movies and live music. In *El Juglar*, 37 Lavapiés you can see and hear Flamenco and jazz, and *El Buscón*, between Calles Sombrerería and Salitre offers hard rock. At *La Campana Café*, 30 Ave María, they serve sweet wine and hot chocolate, and at *Melós* you can have ham and cheese sandwiches. At *Madroños*, 11 Caravaca the specialty is home-made cookies in all flavors.

PLAZA DE SANTA ANA – HUERTAS

There are 60 places of entertainment concentrated in Calle Huertas. Here you will find mostly pubs and cafes with a quieter atmosphere. This is where the 25-40 age group like to go, and the music caters to their taste. To enjoy classical music with a drink in your hand and pleasant company, go to *La Fidula* or *El Capacho*, both at 51 Calle Huertas. You can hear jazz at *Begin the Beguine*, 27 Moratin. At *La Champanería Gala*, 24 Moratin, they serve Spanish and imported champagne. The other places around here are meeting spots for the theater and cinema crowd and for journalists: *La Imprenta*, 27 Magdalena, *La Filmo*, 4 Plaza del Matute, *Sésamo*, 7 Príncipe, *El Café de las Letras*, 37 Santa Maria, *El Reporter*, 6 Fucar and *La Cerveceria Alemana*, 4 Plaza de Santa Ana. They usually close at about 2am, and on Saturdays even later.

PLAZA MAYOR

Here you will find snack bars, bars, exclusive restaurants and Flamenco clubs. The restaurants and snack bars are open until midnight, the bars until 2am; and the Flamenco clubs until the small hours. It's a pleasant and colorful area. The best known Flamenco club is the *Arco de Cuchilleros*, at 7 Cuchilleros.

MALASAÑA

This is a young district which excels in nightlife. As evening approaches you can see the various strange "night types" out on the streets. Most places are open until 3am; Plaza 2 de Mayo is full of life even later than that. *La Manuela*, 29 San Vicente Ferrer, is an old established café, with meetings on important matters open to the public, and jazz and modern music concerts. Another similar café is La *Vía Lactea*,

18 Verlarde. *El Sole de Mayo* and *La Rosa*, which are in the plaza, are favorites with the young, and you can play pool there. At *Damajuana*, 3 Pez and *La Aurora*, 8 Andrés Borrego, you can see plays and pantomime. Although this is usually a noisy district, it does have its relatively quiet niches: *Star*, 25 Plama and *Tetera de la Abuela*, 37 Espíritu Santo, serve tea and cakes in a tranquil atmosphere.

PLAZA DE CHUECA

In this area, old taverns are neighbors of Chinese restau- rants, and there are discos and pubs of all kinds, including gay bars. Outstanding among the old inns is *Angel Sierra*, in Plaza Chueca, which has pre- served its original decor and serves superb snacks. *Pepinil- los*, 63 Los Hortaleza also looks as though time has stood still for it, and there you can have all kinds of stuffed *gherkins* together with wine (the *muscatel* is especially rec- ommended). The discos *Long Play*, 2 Vazquez de Mella, *El Baile*, 2 Reina and *MAC*, 26 Infantas have dance music and alcoholic drinks. In Calle Pelayos are the gay bars:

The Theater Alcázar Nightclub

Leader, *Paralelo*, *Cuero's*, and the *LL-Bar*. *Phalo's* (20 San Marcos) is another. The striptease clubs are also nearby: *Montmartre*, 28 Libertad and *El Poncho Erótico*, 5 San Lorenzo, and in contrast, *A. Doré*, 42 Infantas, serves sandwiches and exhibits modern art.

ALONSO MARTÍNEZ

This fashionable area is the preference of those involved in cinema, fashion, theater and journalism. The most popular places are the old pub, *Nuevo Oliver*, 3 Conde de Xiquene, and *Bocaccio*, 17 Marqués de la Ensenada, which has a disco on the ground floor and a pub upstairs. Open until 4am.

CENTRO AZCA

Concrete and colored lights are the rule here, with innumerable discos and pubs. Between 6-10pm the youngsters arrive, and later on the older generation. The people who come here are an entirely different type to those who frequent the places we have mentioned so far. "Hippies" go to *Malasaña*. At *Huertas* the guests are intellectuals while the artists and Bohemians can be found at *Lavapiés*. You will meet students here, and youngsters from wealthy families. There are bouncers at the doors of the discos, and they inspect everyone, preventing the entry of those who aren't up to standard. For modern music, the discos to go to are

Chapelet, 18 Orense, *Amarello* nearby, and *Verde y Plata*, 22 Orense. At *Samba Boheme*, 22 Orense, it's jacket and tie for the men – and no jeans or sneakers.

Cinema and Theater

As we have said, there are many cinemas in Madrid, and in most of them the soundtrack is dubbed into Spanish.

In the following cinemas the films are shown with their original soundtrack:

Alphaville: 14 Martín de los Heros, Tel. 548-7533. Four cinemas under one roof showing quality films. On Fri. and Sat. they have showings at 12:45am (after midnight).

Bellas Artes: 42 Alcalá, Tel. 532-4652.
Infantas: 21 Infantas.
Filmoteca Nacional: 1 Princessa. Cinematech.

In recent years, theater has flourished in Madrid. Companies are expanding and new theaters are opening. Today there are about 30 theaters in the city of which two are municipal and three are national. In the summer, the theater takes to the streets and there are performances in the parks and squares. The principal theaters are:

Bellas Artes: 42 Alcalá, Tel. 532-4652. Quality theater, special performances. Among the most modern. Closed Wed.

Centro Cultural de la Villa de Madrid: Plaza de Colón, Tel. 575-6080. A very large cultural center belonging to the municipality. Its halls accommodate exhibitions and lectures in addition to the principal activity – theater. (Closed Mon.).

Sala San Pol: Plaza San Pol del Mar, Tel. 541-9089. Madrid's avant garde stage. Sat. and Sun. – plays for children.

Teatro Español: 25 Príncipe, Tel. 429-6297. This is the Spanish National Theater with the oldest tradition. It usually performs classical Spanish plays and those which receive the "Lope de Vega" Award, Spain's most prestigious theatrical award. Closed Mon.

Zarzuela: 4 Jovellanos, Tel. 429-8225. Zarzuela operas and modern dance.

Madrid for Youngsters

Many of the activities arranged by the Madrid Municipality and the district centers are especially for the younger generation. There is plenty to choose from: puppet theaters, plays, painting, sport, hikes and short vacations. All kinds of courses are also available on subjects which, in this day and age, interest even the youngest children: photography, video

and movement, to name but a few.

Most children will enjoy the following outings:

First we suggest a fun-packed one-day tour which adults will also enjoy. It starts at the cable-car at the corner of Calle Marqués de Urquijo and Paseo de Rosales in the Parque del Oeste. The cablecar ride lasts for only 11 minutes (about 1.5 miles), but passes over a particularly lovely part of the city, right into the Casa de Campo.

After the ride, you can visit three sites, each offering its own pleasures. Firstly, there is the zoo, which is quite a good one and fairly large. Its "star" is Cholin, the only panda to be born in captivity. A second attraction is the lake, El Lago, where boats can be hired by the hour. The children can row on the water, while you have a rest in the shade, to the sound of the lapping water. From there, on to the third site, the nearby amusement park with its huge assortment of rides and arcades. For about six dollars you can get a ticket which is good for unlimited use during your visit. At the top of the tower there is a cafeteria, where you can wait for your children.

Those who are not keen on the cablecar can go by metro to Lago, or by bus 33 from Plaza de Isabel II.

On a sunny day the **Retiro**

Park is well worth a visit. There, near the lake, from 10am-3pm, there are shows for children at a minimal price. While the children are watching the puppets, you can walk on and see the Spanish or visiting troupes performing on the promenade. If walking is not what you had in mind, you can sit at one of the bars or gardens around the promenade, and have a drink or a bite to eat. Boats are available for hire at the lake.

If the object of your vacation is to broaden your children's horizons as well as to have fun, you can visit a museum. We have chosen three which would attract any child:

Museo de Carruajes (The Carriage Museum) at Campo del Moro. The entrance is on Paseo Virgen del Puerto. Open Mon.-Sat. 9am-6pm; Sun. and public holidays 9am-3pm.

Museo del Ferrocarril (The Railway Museum) at 61 Paseo de las Delicias. Open Tues.-Sat. 9am-7pm; Sun. and public holidays 9am-2pm.

Museo Naval (The Naval Museum) at 2 Calle Montal-bán. Open 10:30am-1:30pm. Closed on Mon.

Sport

Madrid has a wide selection of sports grounds and clubs, offering a wide range of sports

for active participation or for spectators.

FOOTBALL
Two of Spain's most important soccer clubs are in Madrid: *Real Madrid* and *Atlético de Madrid*, both in the First Division. There are matches every Sunday, at one of two stadiums: Santiago Bernabeu (Real), at Paseo de la Castellana (buses 27, 40, 43; Metro M-3, M-6, M-12); and Vicente Calderón (Atl,tico), reached by metro, stations Pirámides or Marqué de Vadillos.

HORSE-RACING
If you are a horse-racing fan, you can visit the Hipódromo de la Zarzuela on the outskirts of Madrid, on Calle La Coruña. Races are held every Sunday afternoon, with special Metro trains leaving from Noncloa station.

DOG RACING
Dog races are also traditional in Madrid. The Canódromo is at 57 Vía Carpetana, (bus 25). There are races every day, with lots of betting.

SPANISH SQUASH

Another traditional local sport is *Fronto*, a kind of Spanish squash. The central court, the Frontón de Madrid, is at Calle Doctor Cortezo 10 (metro: Teresa de Molina).

SWIMMING

There are several options for swimmers. In the summer heat, the most suitable is the Casa de Campo pool (metro: Lago). In winter, try the heated indoor pool at the La Latina sports center (metro: La Latina). If you really want to spoil yourself and go somewhere exclusive, we suggest the rooftop pool of the *Plaza Hotel*, opposite the Plaza España.

RUNNING

There are three tracks for running – in the Casa Campo, in the Retiro Gardens, and in

Dehesa de la villa, in the northern part of the city.

CYCLING

Every Sunday from 9am-3pm, Calle Príncipe de Vegara is closed to traffic along the stretch between Calles Alcalá and Maria de Molina, and becomes a cycling route. All cyclists are welcome to enjoy themselves.

MOTORSPORTS

On the outskirts of the city there is a motor racing and motorcycle racing track – Jarama – on Calle Borhus, and there are special excursions from Plaza de Castilla on race days.

SKIING

Madrid has something to offer for skiers too: in Navacerrada, about 40 miles from the city, there is a ski resort with all the necessary services. You can get there on the buses of the *La Madrileña* company (opposite the Norte-Príncipe Pío railway station). By car – N-VI to Villalba, exit N-601.

INFORMATION

There are also plenty of private clubs in Madrid, where you can play golf, go horse-riding, or ice-skating. As conditions change, the best way to get up-to-date information, on a particular sport, is to call the information office, Tel. 462-3161.

Congresses and Trade Fairs

In recent years, Madrid has become one of the centers most in demand for the congresses and conventions of international organizations. These meetings are held by all kinds of institutions: the International Red Cross, health and medical organizations, industrial and computer organizations, European institutions and so on. There are even study days on such topics as "Meetings with Creatures from Outer Space".

Such activity demands an infrastructure which includes not only lecture halls, but also suitable hotel accommodation, transport, communications, and good press communication.

For this purpose, a magnificent and comfortable building was erected – the **Palacio de Exposiciones y Congresos** – in Calle General Perón, on the corner of Paseo de la Castellana. The façade of the building is adorned with a huge painting by Joan Miró. Here one can hold nine meetings simultaneously in halls which can seat up to 4,000 people. Concerts and other social functions are also held here. There are also two auditoriums with a capacity for 1,000 or 2,000 people and each one has 200 square meters of exhibition space. There are some smaller conference rooms for smaller groups of people.

In addition to the Palacio de Congresos, 83 hotels offer various services for the organization of congresses for up to 25,000 participants. There are

also some public buildings designated for such meetings.

Madrid's famous trade fairs must also be mentioned. Among them are: The International Tourism Fair (Fitur); The International Fashion Fair (*Intermoda*); The International Book Fair (*Liber*); The Art Fair (Arco) and many more. There are also national Spanish fairs, such as The Jewelry Fair (*Iberjoya*); The Fashion Fair (*Ibermoda*) and the Gift Fair (*Regalo Fama*). These fairs are held in one of two places:

Recinto Ferial de la Casa de Campo, Avenida de Portugal (metro: Lago).

Palacio de las Exposiciones, Paseo de la Castellana 257 (metro: 257 De Castilla).

In order to coordinate the many congresses and activities taking place, information had to be centralized in one office, and so the municipal Oficina de Congresos was established. For detailed information, write or call: Patronato Municipal de Turismo, Oficina de Congresos, C/S 69 Mayor, Madrid 28013, Tel. 588-2900, Fax 588-2930.

For up-to-date information about dates, planning, etc., apply to: *IFEMA*, Juan Carlos I Exhibition Park, Madrid, 28067, Tel. (91)722-5180/722-5000

Filling the Basket: Where to Shop and for What

"Madrid has a store for every kind of merchandise", said the playwright Tirso de Molina in the 17th century, and his words are true to this day. Hundreds of years of commercial and creative activity have left their mark all over the city. Madrid, the capital, is a Spanish

economic center, in particular, but also a European economic center. There are 50,000 shops and stores of every kind in Madrid, and to know your way around for shopping is almost an art in itself.

In the city center, especially in the Gran Vía, the Castellana, the Moncloa and the Salamanca districts there is a large concentration of stores offering everything you can think of.

If you are looking for antiques, the best place is Calle del Prado and its surroundings, especially Plaza de las Cortes and Carrera de San Jerónimo. You can also try the *Rastro* and *Puerta de Toledo*, originally a fish market converted into a shopping center specializing in antiques.

SHOPPING MALLS AND DEPARTMENT STORES

El Corte Inglés: 3 Calle Preciados; 42 Princesa; 79 Raimundo Fernand Villaverde; 76 Goya. Open Mon.-Sat. 10am-9pm.

Galerías Preciados: 1 Plaza del Callao; 10 Arapiles; Magallanes; 87 Goya; 47 Serrano. Open Mon.-Sat. 10am-9pm.

Madrid-2: This is a huge shopping mall in a modern building popularly called "The Ghost Ship". 85,000 sq/m. of commercial space offering the shopper a variety of activities.

There are 350 shops, cafés, restaurants, movie houses,

banks, fast services (e.g., shoe repairs), and games such as bowling. *Madrid-2* is in the La Vaguada district, which you can reach on the Metro, Line 95, or by Bus 67, 83 and 128. There are 3,600 parking places for private cars.

FASHION

Celso Garcia: 2 Conde Peñalver. High quality clothes for men, women and children.

Confecciones Alba: 109 Bravo Murillo. Popular prices.
Don Lope: 18 Arenal. Boutique for ladies' wear.

Elite: 30 Gran Vía. Everything for men. Reasonable prices.

Giggi: 23 Calle Preciados. Fashion for women and girls; reasonable prices.

Jardín de las Modas: 75 Gran Vía. Classic styles for women.

Jesús del Pozo: 28 Almirante. Boutique owned by one of Spain's young and most influential fashion designers.

Loewe: 8 Gran Vía. Clothes, leather goods, and items of current Spanish fashion.

FURS
Del Valle: 4 Conde de Xiquena. High fashion furs and other items.

Manuel Herrero: 7, 23 and 24 Calle Preciados. One of Madrid's best-known furriers.

Marrakesh Export: 25 Plaza Mayor. Specializes in unusual skins and in purses.

FOOTWEAR
Calzados El 10: 22 Carmen. Huge selection. Reasonable prices.

Eureka: 6 Goya; 6 Serrano. High quality designer shoes.

Guerreros: 71 Mayor. Mostly riding boots.

Calzados Esteve: 20 Arenal. Mainly canvas shoes. Reasonable prices.

Iris: 34 Gran Vía. Men's and women's shoes. Average prices.

Los Guerrilleros: 5 Puerta del Sol. Especially low prices.

HANDBAGS, BELTS AND LEATHER GOODS
Galeote: 22 Carmen. Huge selection of purses, bags, etc.

Mayorpiel: 4 Mayor. Bags and suitcases. Reasonable prices.

Meta: 41 Gran Vía. Purses, belts and suitcases.

Vivar: ll Preciados. Purses, shoes and women's fashions.

GIFTS AND MEMENTOS
Comercial Lasarte: 44 Gran Vía. Porcelain and glass items.

Cortes: 7 Preciados. Pens and lighters.

Emylka: 17 Preciados. Jewelry and mementos.

Manacor: 9 Carmen. Typical Spanish art.

Sefarad: 56 Gran Vía. Porcelain pieces, gold and silversmith work from Toledo, local crafts.

JEWELRY
Grassy: 1 Gran Vía. Exclusive

jewelry store with exhibition of old watches.

Joyería Martínez: 26 Carmen.
López: 3 Calle de Prado. Old silver pieces and quality works of art.

Perlas Majorica: 39 Gran Vía. Majorcan pearl art.

Relojeria Fanjul: 8 Carmen.

PERFUMES
Conrado Martín: 16 Mayor. Self-service.

Eduard: 58 Gran Vía. Elegant store for cosmetics, jewelry and fashion.

Marie Young: 26 Carmen. Popular prices.

Perfumería Oriental: 2 Carmen. Wide choice. Reasonable prices.

Perfumería Rosi: 10 and 30 Gran Vía. Huge selection.

Urquiola: 1 Mayor. One of the best known shops for cosmetics and gifts.

SOMETHING SWEET
La Flor de Lis: 11 Puerta del Sol. Candies and sugar-dolls.

The Grassy jewelery store in the Gran Vía

La Pajarita: 6 Puerta del Sol. Special gift-wrapped candies.

La Violeta: 6 Plaza de Canalejas. Small candies with the taste, look and shape of violets.

Casa Mura: 30 Carrera de San Jerónimo. Marzipans, sugared candies, nougat.

Juncal: 15 Recoletos. Chocolates.

ANTIQUES
Alberto Linares: 11 Plaza de las Cortes. Ceramics, paintings and antique jewelry.

Atelier: Galerías Ribera,

Ribera de Curtidores, Tienda 10. Antique jewelry. This gallery contains several antique shops.

Suarte: Calle del Prado. Tapestries, porcelain and antique jewelry.

Centro de Arte y Antiguedades: 5 Serrano.
A complex of 50 art and antique shops.

ELECTRICAL GOODS AND PHOTOGRAPHY

Decoimport: 17 Carmen. Electrical and electronic goods.

Feymar: 6 Gran Vía. Electronic goods and photography equipment.

Foto Frais: Photokin – 41 Alcalá. Photography equipment, developing and printing.

Galeote: Callejón de Precia-dos. Mainly for cinematographers.

Galerías Caraqueñas: 9 Arenal. Rooms full of electrical and electronic goods.

BOOKSTORES

Casa de Libro (Espasa Calpe): 9 Gran Vía. Biggest bookstore in town: five floors of books on varied subjects in several languages.

Fuentetaja: 48 San Bernado. Specializes in social subjects.

Librería Científica General: 38 Preciados. Publicity and photography books.

Librería de la Editora Nacional: 51 Gran Vía. Spanish advertising.

Librería del Patromonio Nacional: 6 Plaza de Oriente. Books on palaces, gardens and Spanish art.

Librería Gaudí: 13 Argensola. Art books.

Crisol: 38 Juan Bravo. Books, discs and newspapers.

MUSICAL INSTRUMENTS AND OTHER MUSICAL REQUISITES

Guitarrería Hnos. Conde: 2 Felipe V. Builder of guitars and other musical instruments.

Real Musical: 1 Carlos III. Everything for the music lover.

Unión Musical Española: 18 Arenal. Musical instruments, scores and records.

Garrido Bailén: 88 Mayor. Builder of musical instruments, especially local ones.

ART GALLERIES
Open usually 11am-2pm and 5pm-8:30pm.

Aele: 28 Claudio Coello, Tel. 575-6679. Entrance from 2 Puigcerdá.

Alencon: 21 Villanueva.

Balboa 13: 13 Nuñez de Balboa.

Collage: 22 Villanueva.

Heller: 13 Claudio Coello, Tel. 435-9102.

Jorge Juán: 11 Jorge Juán, Tel. 575-5098.

Kreisler: 8 Hermosilla, Tel. 431-4264.

La Kábala: 10 Conde de Aranda, Tel. 435-8781.

Skira: 23 José: Ortega y Gasset.

Sokoa: 25 Claudio Coello, Tel. 575-7239.

Torres Begué: Fernan González.

Important Addresses and Phone Numbers

EMERGENCIES
National Police: Tel. 091.
Local Police: Tel. 092.
Traffic Police: Tel. 345-0000.
Ambulance: Tel. 522-2222,
588-4400.
Emergency Medical Services:
Tel. 061.
First Aid: Tel. 588-5103.
Red Cross: Tel. 535-2222.

INFORMATION
Tourist Information
(*Turespaña*): Tel
901-300-600.
Telephone Information
Service: Tel. 003.
Telegrams: Tel. 522-2000.
Telephone Information
Services:
Europe – Tel. 008.
Rest of World – Tel. 089
Central Post Office: Tel.
221-8195
General Information
(Emergency pharmacies,
streets etc.): Tel. 098

In the El Prado Promenade

Metereological Information:
Tel. 094
Sports Information: Tel. 097
Wake up Call: Tel. 096

TRANSPORTATION
Barajas Airport: Tel. 305-8343,
Left Luggage, Tel. 305-3160.
Atocha Railway Station,
Avenida Ciudad de
Barcelona, s/n, Tel.
527-3160.
Chamartín Railway Station,
Agustin de Foxá, s/n, Tel.
323-2121, Left Luggage, Tel.
323-1515.
Norte-Príncipe Pio Railway
Station, 30 Paseo del Rey,
Tel. 547-0000.
Sur Bus Terminal, 17 Canarias,
Tel. 468-4200.
Metro: Tel. 435-2266
Railway Schedules (Renfe):
Tel. 530-0202, Seat Reserva-
tions: Tel. 527-3333.
Taxis:
Radioteléfono Taxi, Tel.
547-8200;
Radio Taxi, Tel.
447-5180;
Tele-Taxi, Tel.
445-9008.
Road Conditions:
Tel. 535-2222.
In-Town Buses (EMT):
Tel. 401-9900
Car-Towing Services:
Tel. 450-1000, 411-1866,
593-3333.

AIRLINES
Air France: 53 Gran Vía, Tel.
542-4900.
Alitalia: 1 Princesa, Tel.
541-8900.
British Airways: 68 Gran Vía,
Tel. 305-4212.

Iberia: 130 Velázquez, Tel.
  587-8787.
KLM: 59 Gran Vía, Tel.
  305-4347.
Delta: 88 Gran Vía, Tel.
  541-4200.
Lufthansa: 88 Gran Vía, Tel.
  305-4240.
TAP: 58 Gran Vía, Tel.
  305-4237.
TWA: 88 Gran Vía, Tel.
  305-4290.

EMBASSIES

Australia: 143 Paseo
  de la Castellana, Tel.
  579-0428.
Canada: 35 Núñez de Balboa,
  Tel. 431-4300.
Great Britain: 16 Fernando
  el Santo, Tel. 319-0200.
South Africa: 91 Claudio
  Coello, Tel. 435-6688.
USA: 75 Serrano, Tel.
  577-4000.

INDEX

INDEX

QUESTIONNAIRE

In our efforts to keep up with the pace and pulse of Madrid, we kindly ask your cooperation in sharing with us any information which you may have, as well as your comments. We would greatly appreciate your completing and returning of the following questionnaire. Feel free to add additional pages.

Our many thanks!

_____

To: Inbal Travel Information (1983) Ltd.
18 Hayetzira st.
Ramat Gan 52521
Israel

Name: _____

Address: _____

Occupation: _____

Date of visit: _____

_____

Purpose of trip (vacation, business, etc.): _____

_____

Comments/Information: _____

_____

_____

_____

_____

_____

_____

_____

INBAL Travel Information Ltd.
P.O.B 1870 Ramat Gan
ISRAEL 52117